Learn and Grow
Hands-On Lessons
For Active Preschoolers

Michelle Caskey

Inquisitive Minds Press®
Caledonia, MI

Learn and Grow: Hands-On Lessons for Active Preschoolers

Published by *Inquisitive Minds Press®*
Caledonia, MI 49316
www.InquisitiveMindsPress.com

Printed in the United States of America

ISBN-10: 0-9885444-0-7
ISBN-13: 978-0-9885444-0-6

Cover and Illustrations by Melanie Rankin

Interior page layout by Michelle L. Caskey

*This book is dedicated to my husband and my best friend. Dennis,
thank-you so much for being willing to be the provider for our family for
all these years. Without your hard work and sacrifice, homeschooling
our boys wouldn't have been possible. I love you!*

Companion Download

This curriculum contains some supplemental material you will want to download for your child. It includes maps, a few worksheets, and other items for you to print for your child to use while completing various lessons throughout this course. To download this material, go to the following website:

http://www.InquisitiveMindsPress.com

If you have never registered at *Inquisitive Minds Press* before, then you will first need to create a new user account by selecting the **Register** link and submitting the necessary information.

Once you have an account and are logged in, select the **Register Products** link. Follow the instructions to register your product.

You will need to use the following password: ***Learningshouldbefun***

Make sure you capitalize the first letter of the password (L). Also make sure that there are no spaces in the password. Select **Register**. Once your product is registered, you may go to **Your Resources** in order to access your companion download.

If you have trouble downloading the supplemental material, send an email to Admin@inquisitivemindspress.com for further assistance, or use the **Contact** page on the website.

www.inquisitivemindspress.com/wp...
....!
PDF - Appendix - Inq.minds Press -
Homeschool your boys.

Learn and Grow:
Hands-On Lessons for Active Preschoolers

Compiled by Michelle Caskey
Illustrated by Melanie Rankin

Introduction

When I first started homeschooling our children, my oldest son was almost two years old. I started out reading to him and doing a few hands-on activities and was completely surprised at how rapidly he progressed. After a few months of working with him, I found myself preparing daily lessons which included English, math, history, science, art, fine or gross motor skills, geography and literature.

I used to spend countless hours researching different topics and projects for us to work on each week. Organizing our schoolwork took me more time than actually teaching it to my son! After a few months, I decided it was time to look for a prepared curriculum we could follow that would save me some time. Unfortunately, I wasn't able to find anything that seemed like real meat and potatoes learning to me. Most preschool curriculums I looked at consisted mainly of crafts and games. Don't get me wrong, there is definitely a place for these types of activities in the life of a preschooler. But they are capable of so much more than what we usually give them credit.

This project has been extremely rewarding for me. It has been a joy to go back through my children's first lessons and to reminisce. I hope that you and your child have as much fun with these lessons as I had with my children! I'd love to hear how you're doing. All the best!

Michelle Caskey
Email: Michelle@homeschool-your-boys.com

A Few Tips Before You Get Started…

Daily Lessons – This curriculum is set up with 26 weeks of lessons. There are projects you can work on with your child five days per week. Be flexible – when you first start out, your child may not be ready to do lessons every day. Feel free to skip a day here and there. Most preschools meet three mornings a week for two year olds and three mornings a week for three year olds. I think you will find that your child will enjoy these lessons and won't want to skip that many days – but use this curriculum as a tool, don't become a slave to it.

Also, don't expect your child to sit down and do all of these activities back to back. Do a few in the morning and a few in the afternoon with play breaks in between. Whenever you sense your child getting tired or frustrated, take a break. One of the goals of schoolwork at this age is to teach your child to love learning… and extra stress and pressure on them won't accomplish this task.

The Library – The library is an amazing resource! If you don't already use the library, be sure to get in there and check it out before starting this curriculum with your child. Ask your librarian how to do interlibrary loans. Many libraries are parts of co-ops so their patrons are able to check out books from a wide variety of libraries – this makes for a huge financial savings for families. And most libraries are connected to the internet so you can search for books and put them on hold in your own home.

In the literature sections of this curriculum, I have recommended books which are related to that week's theme and that my children and I have enjoyed over the years. These books are all available in our library's co-op. Most of them will probably be available to you as well. If not, please search for similar books in your library that are related to the theme. Again, if you need help with this task, you should ask your local librarian.

How Do I Get Started? –

Overall:
1. Look through the entire curriculum.
2. Make a list of needed materials which you don't normally have around the house.
3. You may want to give a copy of this list to all of the grandparents – they are usually eager to help out, either with digging up supplies at home or with helping to purchase some of the school supplies for your child.
4. Begin collecting the necessary materials so that you'll have them when you need them. Try to stay at least a week or two ahead on gathering supplies if possible.

Weekly:
1. Familiarize yourself with one week's lessons at a time.
2. Confirm that all of the necessary materials are available.
3. Complete all of the preparations which are necessary for each lesson.
4. You are ready to start the lessons with your child. Have fun!

Table of Contents

Week One

Your theme for this week will be *apples*. You will be focusing on the following topics with your child:

English –   The letter A
Pre-Math –   Circles and the number 1
Art –   The color red

Lesson One – Monday

English: Recognition of the Letter A

Materials: Card stock
               Apple
               Red paint
               Newspaper
               Paint smock or an old shirt

Preparation: Cut a capital letter A out of card stock.

Lesson:
1. Have your child put on their paint smock or an old shirt to protect their clothing. Have them roll up the sleeves to minimize the mess.
2. While your child is watching, cut the apple in half. Let your child observe what the apple looks like on the inside (the seeds, etc.)
3. Put the paint in a container which is wide enough to easily accommodate the apple. Spread the newspapers out to protect your work surface.
4. Let your child dip their apple into the paint and make apple prints on their capital A. Let their project dry.

Pre-Math – Recognizing Like Objects

Materials: Paper lunch bag
Variety of differently-shaped objects for child to choose from (blocks, etc.) – be sure to include circle shapes and red objects

Preparation: None

Lesson:
1. Spread the block or other objects out on the floor in front of your child.
2. Give your child the paper lunch bag.
3. Tell your child to fill their bag with "all of the circle blocks" or "all of the red blocks", etc.
4. As your child puts each object into the bag, have them explain why it belongs in there.

Art – Hand Apple Tree

Materials: Construction Paper
Brown, Red, Yellow and Green Paint
Paint brush

Preparation: None

Lesson:
1. Let your child paint one of their hands brown.
2. Help them press their hand with outstretched fingers onto the construction paper to make the tree trunk.
3. Have your child wash their hands.
4. Then give your child the red, yellow and green paint as well as any other supplies you choose.
5. Let your child create their own version of an apple tree.

Gross Motor Skills – Apple Toss

Materials: Laundry Basket or Bushel Basket
               Red Bean Bags or soft red balls
               Masking tape

Preparation: Use the masking tape to create a line on the floor. Place the basket a
               couple of feet behind the line.

Lesson:
1. Have your child stand behind the line and try to toss the "apples" into the basket.
2. Have them try throwing overhand, underhand, while standing backwards, etc.
   Come up with as many variations as you can think of.
3. Continue to let them play this until they grow tired of the game.

Science – How Many Apples Tall Am I?

Materials: Several apples
               Tape measure

Preparation: None

Lesson:
1. Have your child lay down on the ground.
2. Measure how tall they are by using apples. If you don't have enough apples to
   equal the length of your child, take apples from the beginning of the measurement
   and move them to the end in a leap frog method as you continue your counting.
3. After you know how many apples tall your child is, you may want to measure
   them with the tape measure and let them know how tall they are in feet and
   inches.
4. Then lay down on the ground and let your child measure how tall you are with the
   apples and/or tape measure. They will love this!

Literature:
Apples Here! by Will Hubbell
Autumn is for Apples by Michelle Knudsen
Up, Up, Up! It's Apple-Picking Time by Jody Fickes Shapiro
The Apple Pie Tree by Zoe Hall

Lesson Two – Tuesday

English: Recognition of the Color Red

Materials: Picture of Fox (see companion download)
              Red construction paper or tissue paper
              Glue Stick

Preparation: Print the picture of the fox from the companion download onto a large
              piece of paper.

Lesson:
1. Give your child the red construction paper or tissue paper.
2. Talk to them about what color it is over and over while they work on their picture.
3. Let them rip the construction paper or tissue paper into small pieces and glue it onto the picture of the fox.
4. Let your child be the one to use the glue stick. As they first start working with a glue stick it will be messy – but with your guidance they will quickly be able to master this skill.

Pre-Math: Fractions

Materials: Two red apples

Preparation: None

Lesson:
1. Show your child the whole apples.
2. Cut one apple in half and explain to them that you have cut the apple in half. You have two halves.
3. Cut one of the halves in half. Explain to them that you now have two quarters.
4. Cut one of the quarters in half. Explain to them that you now have two eighths.
5. Let them see the difference between a whole, a half, a quarter, and a eighth.
6. Put all of the pieces back together to show your child how each of these smaller pieces make up the whole apple.
7. Go ahead and enjoy eating some apple with your child.

Art – Stained Glass Apple

Materials: Contact Paper or Waxed Paper
Red Tissue paper or construction paper
Leaves (optional)
Brown Yarn
Glue Stick

Preparation: Cut the contact paper or waxed paper into two identical apple shapes per child.

Lesson:
1. Give your child one contact paper apple.
2. Let them use the tissue paper, construction paper and leaves to make their own apple creations.
3. They can be as creative as they would like. They can use the yarn to make a worm in the apple if they would like.
4. After their apple looks the way they would like it, give the other contact paper apple shape to your child and let them glue it to the back of their creation. Help them to glue a loop of brown yarn at the top of their apples.
5. After they have dried, let your child hang their apple in the window.

Fine Motor Skills – Lacing Apples

Materials: Picture of apple (see companion download)
Poster board
Thin Shoestring
Hole Puncher

Preparation:
1. Print the apple from the companion download onto a piece of poster board.
2. Laminate the apple.
3. Use the hole puncher to punch holes around the edges of the apple.
4. Tie the shoestring to one of the holes

Lesson:
1. Give your child the apple and string.
2. Show them how to lace the apple. This is great for developing their fine motor skills.
3. Let them lace and unlace the apple as many times as they are willing.

Literature:
Clifford's First Autumn by Norman Bridwell
Fletcher and the falling leaves by Julia Rawlinson
White Rabbit's Color Book by Alan Baker
A is for Adam by Ken and Molly Ham

Lesson Three – Wednesday

English: Play Hide the A

Materials: Red Card stock or construction paper

Preparation: Cut a large, capital and a large lowercase
                letter A out of the card stock or construction paper.

Lesson:
1. Hide the letters somewhere. Begin by hiding the letters out in the open, then slightly camouflage them if your child's ability allows.
2. Try to put the letters near objects which begin with the letter A.
3. Talk to your child about the sounds that the letter A makes.
4. Let your child look for the letters. Tell them if they're getting warmer if they get closer or colder if they get farther away.
5. After they find the letters, see if they can identify the object near the letter which begins with the letter A.

Pre-Math – Counting Apple Seeds

Materials: Apple Core picture (see companion download)
                Card stock or construction paper
                Black construction paper

Preparation:
1. Print the apple core on the card stock or construction paper.
2. Cut five small round circles out of the black construction paper to use as apple seeds.
3. Laminate everything if you want your child to be able to practice these skills all week.

Lesson:
1. Give your child the apple core and a handful of "seeds".
2. Ask them to put different numbers of seeds on their apple. Use the numbers 0 – 5.
3. Emphasize the number one as that is the focus number of the week.
4. Continue to have your child put different amounts of seeds on their apple core until they tire of the activity.

Geography/History: Johnny Appleseed

Materials: Map of United States (see
                   companion download)
                   Johnny Appleseed by Patricia Demuth
                   Crayons

Preparation: Print the map from the companion download.

Lesson:
1. Read Johnny Appleseed by Patricia Demuth to your child.
2. Give them the map of the United States.
3. Point out which state they live in on the map.
4. Let our child color that state.
5. Point out the states where Johnny Appleseed traveled and planted apples (Illinois, Indiana, Kentucky, Pennsylvania and Ohio.)
6. Let your child color those states red.

Gross Motor Skills – Apple Relay

Materials: a red apple

Preparation: None

Lesson:
1. Give your child the apple.
2. Have them run to a designated spot and run back.
3. If you have two or more children they can hand the apple back and forth as they run. If you are working with one child, you can take turns running with the apple.
4. Let your child take several turns at this game. It will help them to burn off excess energy so that they will be able to concentrate better on your next activity.

Science – Apple Survey

Materials: Several different types of apples

Preparation: None

Lesson:
1. Let your child try tasting several different types of apples to see which ones they like the best.
2. You can have them try several types in one day – or spread this activity over the entire week and let them try a different apple each day.

11

Literature:

Apples and oranges : going bananas with pairs by Sara Pinto
We all fall for apples by Emmi S. Herman
God must really love colors by Rondi DeBoer
Circles Around Town by Nathan Olson

Lesson Four – Thursday

English: Go to the Library

Materials: None

Preparation: None

Lesson:
1. Go to the library.
2. Let your child pick out some books that he or she might enjoy.
3. Reading is so important! You should do everything you can to get your child excited about reading at a young age.

Pre-Math – Counting Apples

Materials: Brown, green, and red felt
White construction paper

Preparation:
1. Make three apple trees and several apples from the felt.
2. Make number cards 0-5 with the white construction paper.
3. You can laminate these number cards to use in subsequent lessons if you would like.

Lesson:
1. Give your child the apple trees and apples.
2. Put different number cards under each tree.
3. Have your child put the correct number of apples on each tree.

Art/Music – Apple Tambourine

Materials: 2 Paper plates per child
Red paint
Paint brushes
Tacky Glue
Stapler
Noise makers (bells, buttons, small pebbles, etc)
Red ribbon
Toddlin' Tunes – Sing Along with Cathy Bollinger (or other music CD)

Preparation: None

Lesson:
1. Let your child paint the outsides of two paper plates.
2. After the paint has dried, let them put your noise makers of choice on one of the plates.
3. Assist your child in gluing and stapling the two plates together.
4. Staple a flowing piece of red ribbon to the plates.
5. Let the child use their apple tambourine while listening to and dancing with music.

Fine Motor Skills – Apple Match

Materials: Green, yellow and red construction paper
Three plastic bowls
Tape

Preparation:
1. Cut out apple shapes from the green, yellow and red construction paper.
2. Tape one of each color apple to the outside of one of the bowls.

Lesson:
1. Mix up the different colored apples and spread them out in front of your child.
2. Let your child sort the apples into the proper bowls.

Literature:
Apples add up! by Megan E. Bryant and Monique Z. Stephens
Red are the apples by Marc Harshman and Cheryl Ryan
How Do Dinosaurs Learn Their Colors? by Jane Yolen
Circles by Marybeth Lorbiecki

Lesson Five – Friday

English: Achoo Game

Materials: Berenstain's A Book by Stan & Jan Berenstain

Preparation: None

Lesson:
1. Explain to your child that one of the sounds the letter A makes is AH.
2. Explain to them that you're going to read a book to them. Every time they hear you use the AH sound, they need to pretend to sneeze ("achoo").
3. Read the Berenstain's A Book to your child.
4. Whenever you find yourself saying a word that has the AH sound in it, pause a bit to cue your child to say "Achoo."

Pre-Math – Candy Land

Materials: Candy Land game

Preparation: None

Lesson:
1. Play Candy Land with your child.
2. Be sure to let your child identify the colors on the cards and the game board as often as they possibly can.
3. If your child seems hesitant to identify the color red, encourage them that they know this color as they have been studying it all week.

Art – Johnny Appleseed Picture

Materials: Johnny Appleseed coloring page (see companion download)

Preparation: Print the Johnny Appleseed coloring page for your child.

Lesson:
1. Let your child color the coloring page.
2. If they don't act interested in coloring, be sure to sit down with them and help them to color. Kids enjoy doing things with you more than they will enjoy them on their own.

Gross Motor Skills – Bobbing for Apples

Materials: Large bucket or barrel
               Small apples or apple slices
               Blindfold (optional)

Preparation: Fill the bucket with water.

Lesson:
1. If it's a warm, sunny day you may want to do this one outside.
2. Put the apples or apple slices in the water.
3. Have your child put their hands behind their back.
4. Have your child try to get an apple or an apple slice out of the water using just their teeth.
5. If your child gets too frustrated without being able to use their hands, go ahead and let them use their hands to guide the apple to their mouth.
6. Be prepared that your child may want you to go first so you can show them how to do this.
7. This is a great way to cool off on a warm Indian Summer day.

Literature:
From apples to applesauce by Kristin Thoennes Keller
One Tractor : A Counting Book by Alexandra Siy
Max and Mo Go Apple Picking by Patricia Lakin
In the leaves by Huy Voun Lee

Week Two

Your theme for this week will be *bubbles*. You will be focusing on the following topics with your child:

English – The letter B
Pre-Math – Circles and the number 1
Art – The color blue

_____

Lesson Six – Monday

English: Capital Letter B

Materials: Card stock
               Dried beans
               Glue

Preparation: Cut a capital B out of the card stock.

Lesson:
1. Give your child their letter.
2. While working on this project, talk to them about how this is the letter B and about what sound it makes.
3. Depending on the maturity of your child, you may need to help them with the glue. You or they can squirt glue on a large patch of the letter.
4. Let your child place beans on their letter B.

Pre-Math – Sorting Everyday Objects

Materials: A variety of socks (some white, some colored, some big, some small)

Preparation: None

Lesson:
1. Start separating the socks into two different groups.
2. Ask your child how the items in each group are alike. How are they different?
3. Give your child one more object and ask them which group that object should be put in and why?
4. Put socks together into one pile and let your child try to sort them by whatever criteria you choose.
5. If you have blue socks in the pile, be sure to point them out to your child as that is the color of the week.

Art – Bubble Picture

Materials: White construction paper
               Blue construction paper
               Glue stick
               Crayons

Preparation: Cut out various sizes of circles from the white construction paper.

Lesson:
1. Give your child the blue construction paper and the white circles.
2. Let them glue the circles (bubbles) to their paper however they would like to make a bubble picture.
3. Let your child color their paper when they are done gluing.

Gross Motor Skills – Balloons

Materials: Balloons
               Laundry basket or box

Preparation: Blow up several balloons and put them in the laundry basket or box until you're ready to use them.

Lesson:
1. Let your child pick a balloon out of the box and play with it.
2. Practice batting the balloon in the air and letting your child try to bat it as well.

Science – Water Bubbles versus Milk Bubbles

Materials: Two glasses
                  Two straws
                  Water
                  Milk
                  A bath towel

Preparation: None

Lesson:
1. Pour some milk into one glass and some water into the other.
2. Put the straws in the glasses.
3. Give your child the glass with water and instruct them to blow in their glass. They will be able to get their water to bubble.
4. Now give your child the glass with milk.
5. Wrap the towel tightly around their glass and instruct them to blow in their straw. They will be delighted when they see the milk bubble up and over the side of their glass.

Literature:
Clifford Counts Bubbles by Norman Bridwell
The turn-around upside-down alphabet book by Lisa Campbell Ernst
The Berenstains' B book by Stanley and Janice Berenstain
A circle in the sky by Zachary Wilson

Lesson Seven – Tuesday

English: Blind Pick

Materials: Poster board or large piece of construction paper
                          Thick blue marker

Preparation: Write several different numbers (0-5), letters (A-E), and shapes (circle, square, and triangle) on the poster board with the marker.

Lesson:
1. Have your child cover their eyes and point at the poster board.
2. See if your child can identify whatever number, letter or shape at which they are pointing.
3. Do this several times until they have identified a variety of objects.
4. If they haven't pointed to the numbers 1 & 2, the letters A & B and a circle individually point these out and have them identify them as they are the ones you have been focusing on so far.

Pre-Math – Number Scramble

Materials: Card stock
                          Black or blue marker

Preparation: Cut the card stock into five cards. Write the numbers 1-5 on the cards.

Lesson:
1. Scramble up the cards and see if your child can put them in order.
2. If they are really struggling with this task, try giving them only numbers 1 and 2 since those are the numbers you've been focusing on so far.
3. Then add in additional numbers one by one and have them put them in order, etc.
4. You may want to laminate these cards and save them to be used in subsequent lessons.

Music – Balloon Bounce

Materials: Balloons (can use the balloons from last week if you still have any)
                          Laundry basket or empty box
                          Smile a Little: 15 Fun Songs for Little Ones or other CD of your choice

Preparation: Blow up some balloons and put them in the laundry basket or box.

Lesson:
1. Turn on the music.
2. Let your child try to bounce balloons to the music.

Fine Motor Skills – Drawing Circles

Materials: Paper
                 Crayons
                 Yellow highlighter (optional)

Preparation: None

Lesson:
1. Give your child some paper and crayons.
2. Instruct them to practice drawing circles on their paper.
3. If they are struggling with this skill, try drawing some circles on the paper with the yellow highlighter and letting them trace them.
4. Once they feel comfortable, they can try to draw some circles on their own.

Science – Bubble Mountains

Materials: Plastic bowl
                 Water
                 Liquid soap
                 Straw
                 Newspapers

Preparation:
1. Put the water and liquid soap in the bowl.
2. Cover the table with newspapers.

Lesson:
1. Give your child the straw.
2. Be sure they understand how to blow out with their straw.
3. Tell them it's important not to suck in with their straw.
4. After they have demonstrated this skill with their straw, have them put the straw in their bowl and blow. This will cause bubbles to form and make bubble mountains.

Literature:
Monster Bubbles : a counting book by Dennis Nolan
God made shapes-- for me! by Christine Tangvald
Little smudge by Lionel Le Néouanic
Shape capers by Cathryn Falwell

Lesson Eight – Wednesday

English – My B Balloon

Materials: Balloon
                Old magazines or newspaper inserts
                Scissors
                Tacky Glue

Preparation: None

Lesson:
1. Help your child to look through the magazines and find pictures of objects that start with a B.
2. Blow up the balloon for your child.
3. Let your child glue the "B" pictures onto the balloon.
4. Then let them play with the balloon. You can bat the balloon back and forth and say "BUH" (the sound that B makes.)

Pre-Math – Shape Matching

Materials: Various colors of construction paper

Preparation: Cut out various sizes and colors of circles, squares, triangles, rectangles and diamonds. You may want to laminate these shapes so that they can be used in subsequent lessons.

Lesson:
1. Put the shapes on the floor in front of your child.
2. Have your child match the shapes - first by size, then by color and finally by shape.

Art – Bubble Wrap Painting

Materials: Bubble wrap
Construction paper
Blue paint
Wide, shallow container

Preparation:
1. Make the bubble wrap into a glove by folding it over and stapling it together.
2. Pour the paint into the wide, shallow container.

Lesson:
1. Give your child their construction paper, the paint and their bubble wrap glove.
2. Let them dip their glove into the paint and press it onto their construction paper.
3. Let them make whatever type of bubble picture they would like.

Gross Motor Skills – Bubble Sheet Stomping

Materials: Bubble wrap

Preparation: None

Lesson:
1. Put large sheets of bubble wrap on the floor and let your child jump all over it.
2. See if they can pop all of the bubbles.
3. They will love it if you will jump on the bubble wrap with them.

Science – Bubble Observation

Materials: Bubble solution and a wand

Preparation: None

Lesson:
1. Let your children go outside and blow some bubbles.
2. Point out that the bubbles aren't all the same size and they don't all behave in the same way.
3. What happens if they blow hard?
4. How about if they blow softly?
5. What color are bubbles?
6. Are all bubbles the same shape?
7. If they touch a bubble what happens?
8. How long do bubbles last?

Literature -
Ship shapes by Stella Blackstone
Benny's big bubble by Jane O'Connor
Bubble trouble by Stephen Krensky
The smushy bus by Leslie Helakoski

Lesson Nine – Thursday

English – My Placemat

Materials: Construction paper
                 Crayons or markers
                 Yellow highlighter
                 Contact paper

Preparation: Write your child's name on their placemat with the yellow highlighter.

Lesson:
1. Let your child make a placemat with their name on it.
2. Have your child trace their name.
3. Have them decorate their placemats however they'd like.
4. Cover their placemat with contact paper and let them use it at mealtime. This will help them to recognize their name more quickly.

Pre-Math – Dominoes

Materials: Dominoes

Preparation: None

Lesson: Have your child match the dot patterns on the dominoes. Depending on the age and ability of your child, you may be able to play an actual game of dominoes with them.

Geography – Map of House

Materials: <u>Me on the Map</u> by Joan Sweeney
                 Paper
                 Crayons

Preparation: None

Lesson:
1. Read <u>Me on the Map</u> to your child.
2. Help them to make a map of their house.

Fine Motor Skills – Puzzles

Materials: Puzzles

Preparation: None

Lesson: Let your child put together a few puzzles. Puzzles are good for fine motor skills as well as hand-eye coordination.

Literature:
Thing! by Mick Inkpen
What can Simon be? by Gene Yates
'Round and around by James Skofield
Round is a pancake by Joan Sullivan Baranski

Lesson Ten – Friday

English – Tracing a B

Materials: Card stock
                  Paper
                  Pencil

Preparation: Write the letter B on the card stock.

Lesson:
1. Put the paper over the card with the letter B.
2. Let your child trace the B with a pencil.
3. An alternative way to do this is to tape the card and the paper to a window on a sunny day and let your child trace the B that way.

Pre-Math – Counting

Materials: None

Preparation: None

Lesson:
1. Count while your child is getting dressed this morning.
2. Be sure to count out loud and evenly "1 second, 2 seconds, etc."
3. Children will hear numbers which will help them learn to count, and they will begin to develop a sense of duration.

Art – Finger Painting

Materials: Blue finger paint
                  Large piece of construction paper

Preparation: None

Lesson:
1. Let your child finger paint.
2. They can come up with any creation they desire. Some children will try to make a picture and some will just dip their fingers in the paint and smear them around for the tactile experience. Let your child work at their own pace.

Gross Motor Skills – Bean Bag Toss

Materials: A Beanbag (blue, if you have one)

Preparation: None

Lesson:
1. Play catch with your child.
2. Start out close together and slowly move farther apart.
3. Try playing catch standing up as well as sitting down.
4. If your child throws a wild one, let them retrieve it – this will help them to burn off some of their excess energy.

Science – Bubble Me

Materials: 2/3 cup Joy dishwashing liquid
1 gallon water
2-3 Tbsp glycerin (available in the pharmacy)
Wading pool
Hula hoop

Preparation: Make the homemade bubble solution by mixing the dishwashing liquid, the water, and the glycerin. Use it to fill the wading pool (several inches deep.)

Lesson:
1. Place the hula hoop in the pool.
2. Let your child step inside the hula hoop.
3. Slowly pull the hula hoop over their head.
4. Your child will be standing inside a giant bubble.

Literature -
Squarehead by Harriet Ziefert
Rolie Polie Olie by William Joyce
Circle song by Diana Engel
Circles by Janie Spaht Gill

Week Three

Your theme for this week will be *cows and other domesticated animals*. You will be focusing on the following topics with your child:

English – The letter C
Pre-Math – Squares and the number 2
Art – The color brown

Lesson Eleven – Monday

English – Recognition of the Letter C

Materials: Card stock
                 Stalk of celery
                 Brown paint
                 Newspaper
                 Paint smock or an old shirt

Preparation: Cut a capital letter C out of card stock.

Lesson:
1. Have your child put on their paint smock or an old shirt to protect their clothing.
2. Have them roll up the sleeves to minimize the mess.
3. Put the paint in a container. Spread the newspapers out to protect your work surface.
4. Let your child dip their celery into the paint and make prints on their capital letter C.
5. Let their project dry.

Pre-Math – Shape Sort

Materials: Shapes created in lesson 8

Preparation: None

Lesson:
1. Spread out the various shapes in front of your child.
2. Start with a square since this is the shape we're focusing on this week.
3. Ask your child the following questions about each shape:
   a. How many sides does this shape have?
   b. Are the sides straight?
   c. What is the name of this shape?
   d. Does the shape look the same if I turn it this way? How does it change?

Art – Milk Carton Cow Barn

Materials: Empty milk carton
               Red or brown paint
               Newspapers
               Paper (optional)

Preparation: Cut doors into the milk carton. Put down newspapers on the work surface.

Lesson:
1. Give the milk carton to your child.
2. Let them paint the milk carton to make it look like a barn.
3. Depending on the ability and interest of your child, you can also let them paint a picture of a cow on a separate sheet of paper.

Gross Motor Skills – Animal Acting

Materials: None

Preparation: None

Lesson:
1. Have your child act like different animals.
   a. Have them walk like a cow (crawl on all fours.)
   b. Have them slither like a snake.
   c. Have them do the crab walk.
   d. Have them gallop like a horse, etc.

Science – Homemade Butter

Materials: Baby food or other small jar
                   Heavy whipping cream
                   Marble (optional)

Preparation: None

Lesson:
1. Talk to your child about all of the different kinds of foods you get from a farm (milk, meat, eggs, vegetables, fruits, etc.)
2. Talk about the different products that are made from milk (ice cream, cottage cheese, yogurt, cheese, butter, etc.)
3. Put some whipping cream in a jar and let your child shake it vigorously. Putting a marble inside the jar as well speeds up the process.
4. Once the butter is formed, let your child try some on a piece of toast.

Literature -
Arthur's tractor by Pippa Goodhart
Ah-choo! by Margery Cuyler
Baa! Moo! : what will we do? by A. H. Benjamin
Bernard the angry rooster by Mary Wormell

Lesson Twelve – Tuesday

English – Name Bingo

Materials: Markers
                Paper
                Alphabet flash cards (can be homemade)
                Stickers

Preparation: None

Lesson:
1. Have your child write his or her name on a piece of paper. If your child struggles with this task, write their name on the paper in yellow marker and let them trace it.
2. You may want to write your name down on a separate sheet of paper and play this game with your child as well.
3. Draw one flash card at a time and let your child try to identify the letter.
4. When a letter is drawn that is in your child's name, they get to cross out that letter on their paper.
5. Do this until all of the letters in their name are crossed out.
6. When your child has crossed out their entire name, they earn a sticker.

Pre-Math – Fill the Squares

Materials: Sheet of Stickers
                Paper

Preparation: Draw a large grid of squares on the paper.

Lesson:
1. Give a sheet of stickers to your child.
2. Let them peel off their own stickers and place one in each square.

Music – Peter and the Wolf

Materials: "Peter and the Wolf" music CD w/ narration

Preparation: None

Lesson:
1. Listen to the CD.
2. Help your child try to identify the different musical instruments that represent the characters in the story.

Fine Motor Skills – Drawing Practice

Materials: Crayons or pencil
                Paper

Preparation: None

Lesson:
1. Let your child practice drawing squares on a piece of paper.
2. If they struggle with this skill, start out by using a yellow marker to draw a few squares and let them trace them. Then help your child progress to drawing squares on their own.

Literature -
Big red barn by Margaret Wise Brown
Biscuit's day at the farm by Alyssa Satin Capucilli
Blue Goose by Nancy Tafuri.
Book! book! book! by Deborah Bruss

Lesson Thirteen – Wednesday

English – Alphabetical Order

Materials: A, B and C Flashcards

Preparation: None

Lesson:
1. Let your child try to put the flashcards in alphabetical order.
2. Mix them up and have them try it again. Let them continue until they can do it quickly without struggling.

Pre-Math – Shape Scavenger Hunt

Materials: None

Preparation: None

Lesson:
1. Do a scavenger hunt for shapes.
2. This hunt can take place at home, at the park, in the car, or in a store.
3. Try to identify lots of squares as that is the shape we're focusing on this week.

Art – Marble Cow

Materials: Brown paint
               Crayons or markers
               Construction paper
               Cow picture (see companion download)
               Glue stick

Preparation:
1. Print the cow shape from the companion download.
2. Cut out the cow for your child.

Lesson:
1. Let your child glue their cow onto the construction paper.
2. Using the brown paint, let them paint spots on the cow.
3. Your child can then use the crayons or markers to draw a barn.

Gross Motor Skills – Galloping

Materials: None

Preparation: None

Lesson: Let your child pretend to be a galloping horse.

Science – Milk a Cow

Materials: Latex glove
                Water or milk
                Bucket

Preparation: Poke small holes in the fingers of the glove.

Lesson:
1. Remind your children where milk comes from.
2. Holding the glove over the bucket, fill the glove with water or milk.
3. Let your child milk the cow (pull on the fingers of the glove.)

Literature -
Carrot in my pocket by Kitson Flynn
A chick called Saturday by Joyce Dunbar
Chicken bedtime is really early by Erica S. Perl
Chickens to the rescue by John Himmelman

Lesson Fourteen – Thursday

English – Clothes on the Clothesline

Materials: Catalog or old magazine
                  String
                  Pinching clothespins

Preparation:
1. Cut out pictures of clothing from the catalog.
2. Print a letter on each piece of clothing – mostly capital and lowercase C's – but include some A's and B's as well.
3. Hang up the string to use as a clothesline (be sure it is low enough that your child can easily reach it.)

Lesson:
1. Spread out the pictures of clothes in front of your child.
2. Tell them to choose all of the clothes which have a letter C on them and hang them up on the clothesline.
3. Try to let your child do this on their own as much as possible.
4. Once they think they have them all hung up, prompt them if they have forgotten any.

Pre-Math – Number Scramble

Materials: Number Cards 1-5

Preparation: None

Lesson:
1. Scramble the number cards.
2. Place them face up in front of your child.
3. See if they can put the cards in numerical order.
4. If your child really struggles with this activity, start out by giving them just 1 and 2 and have them put those two in order. Then you can add further numbers one at a time and see if they are able to put them in order.

Geography – My Map

Materials: Paper
               Crayons and pencil

Preparation: None

Lesson:
1. Go on a walk with your child.
2. Observe three different objects that are near your home. These can be other houses, trees, mailboxes, etc.
3. Go back home and help your child draw a map that includes your house and the three objects you both decided upon.
4. Then go for another walk bringing your map with you to see if you drew the objects in the correct places.

Fine Motor Skills – Preschooler Sprinkling

Materials: Empty milk jug
               Hammer and nail

Preparation: Use the hammer and nail to poke holes in the bottom of the milk jug.

Lesson:
1. Go outside with your child.
2. Fill up the jug with water and let your child use it to sprinkle the grass, flowers, the sidewalk, etc.

Literature
Chicks and salsa by Aaron Reynolds
Chuck's truck by Peggy Perry Anderson
Cow in the dark by Todd Aaron Smith
The cow that went oink by Bernard Most

Lesson Fifteen – Friday

English – Shape Tracing

Materials: Paper
                    Glue
                    Colored sand or glitter
                    Scissors

Preparation: None

Lesson:
1. Draw two or three squares on a piece of paper.
2. Have your child squeeze out glue around the edges of each square.
3. Help your child hold their paper over a wastebasket. Then let them sprinkle colored sand or glitter on top of the glue.
4. Help them to shake off the excess sand/glitter.

Pre-Math – Pairs

Materials: Old magazines or a catalog

Preparation: None

Lesson:
1. Sit down with your child and look through old magazines or a catalog.
2. Help them to find pictures of things that come in twos (i.e., shoes, socks, eyes, ears, feet, bike wheels, suspenders, gloves, etc.
3. (Optional) If you'd like, you can have your child cut out these items and glue them to a piece of construction paper to make a collage of pairs.

Art – Legless Cows

Materials: Shape of a cow without legs (see companion download)
                    2 Snap clothespins
                    Crayons
                    Paint (Optional)

Preparation: Print the cow from the companion download.

Lesson:
1. Let your child color the cow.
2. Your child can paint the clothespins to match their cow if you would like.
3. After the legs dry, have your child put the "legs" on their cow.

Gross Motor Skills – Rolling

Materials: Soft mat or rug (optional)

Preparation: None

Lesson: Let your child roll back and forth on the floor or on a mat.

Science – Texture Touch

Materials: Various textured material (i.e., sandpaper, old carpeting, fabric, cotton balls, fur, etc.)
Lids from cans of frozen juice

Preparation: Glue the various materials to the backs of the lids.

Lesson:
1. Let your child experience the different textures.
2. Let your child sort the textures from smoothest to roughest, etc.

Literature
The cows are in the corn by James Young
Cows in the kitchen by June Crebbin
Digby takes charge by Caroline Jayne Church
Floss by Kim Lewis

Week Four

Your theme for this week will be *dogs and other pets*. You will be focusing on the following topics with your child:

English – The letter D
Pre-Math – Squares and the number 2
Art – The color black

Lesson Sixteen – Monday

English: Recognition of the Letter D

Materials: Card stock
              Circle stickers (dots)
              Crayons

Preparation: Cut a capital letter D out of card stock.

Lesson:
1. Let your child color their D.
2. Give them some dot stickers and let them stick them all over their letter.

Pre-Math – Brown Collage

Materials -   Old animal magazines
              Construction paper
              Scissors
              Glue stick

Preparation: None

Lesson:
1. Give your child some old magazines to go through.
2. Have them look for pictures of brown animals.
3. Cut your child cut out the brown animals and glue them to their construction paper to make a collage of brown animals.

Art – Paper Plate Aquarium

Materials: Tissue paper
               Construction paper
               Googly eyes
               Yarn
               Markers
               Scissors
               Glue
               Plastic disposable plate
               Plastic wrap
               Masking tape (optional)

Preparation: None

Lesson:
1. Give your child a paper plate.
2. Let them use the art supplies to make an aquarium scene on their plate.
3. Stretch plastic wrap over the top of the plate (you may need to tape it into place). This will make it look like you're looking into an aquarium.

Gross Motor Skills – Balancing

Materials: Various materials to balance (i.e., book, ball, hat, plastic cup, umbrella, plastic plate, toy figure, etc.)

Preparation: None

Lesson:
1. Tell your child they will be reading a book called The Cat in the Hat a little bit later. In this book, the cat balances a lot of different objects.
2. Tell your child they are going to try to balance some items and see which ones are easy and which ones are difficult.
3. Let them try to balance a variety of objects on their hand, on their head, on a lifted foot, etc.

Science – Make a Pet

Materials: Newspaper
               Paper lunch bag
               Tape or rubber band
               Markers
               Construction paper
               Yarn
               Glue
               Scissors

Preparation: None

Lesson:
1. Tell your child they are going to make their own pet.
2. Have them tear the newspaper into strips, crumple them up and stuff them into the paper lunch bag until the bag is nearly full. Help your child close the bag with tape or a rubber band.
3. Then let your child make a face on their bag with markers or bits of construction paper. They can also add ears, whiskers, paws, or tails.
4. Let your child name their pet.
5. Help your child tie on a yarn leash and they can take their pet for a walk.

Literature –
    The Cat in the Hat by Dr. Seuss
    Patches Lost and Found by Steven Kroll
    Bad Dog, Marley! by John Grogan
    Good dog, Carl by Alexandra Day

Lesson Seventeen – Tuesday

English – Finish the Animals

Materials: Unfinished animal patterns (see companion download)
Construction paper
Various sizes and colors of clips and clothespins
Card stock
Crayons and markers
Glue stick

Preparation:
1. Make copies of the unfinished animal patterns on card stock.
2. Depending on the abilities of your child, you may want to cut out the animal patterns for them in advance as well.

Lesson:
1. Provide your child with the animals and the art supplies.
2. Let your child decorate the animals however they desire.
3. Let them use the various clips and clothespins for legs, tails and ears.

Pre-Math – Potato Prints

Materials: 2 potatoes
Paint (be sure to include black paint)
Construction Paper

Preparation: Cut a circle, a triangle, a rectangle and a square into four potato halves.

Lesson:
1. Let your child dip the potato shapes into the paint and let them make whatever kind of picture they would like on their construction paper.
2. Get a new piece of paper and make a shape pattern alternating two different shapes.
3. Ask your child to copy the pattern.
4. As your child is working, ask them the following:
    a. What are the names of the shapes?
    b. Which shape comes first?
    c. What pattern do you see?
    d. Ask your child to continue the pattern.

Geography – My City

Materials: A map of your city
                   A marker

Preparation: None

Lesson:
1. Look at a map of your city with your child.
2. Try to identify at least 3 different locations to which you go on a regular basis.
3. Let your child circle them.
4. Then help your child to trace the route from your house to these locations.
5. Use your map to drive to these different locations. Help your child to navigate if they are able.

Fine Motor Skills – Pet Home Match

Materials: Pet Home Match worksheet (see companion download)
                   Pencil

Preparation: Print the Pet Home Match worksheet from the companion download.

Lesson:
1. Give the worksheet to your child.
2. Have them draw a line to match the animals to their homes.

Literature -
Officer Buckle and Gloria by Peggy Rathmann
Harry, the dirty dog by Gene Zion
But no elephants by Jerry Smath
Albert, the dog who liked to ride in taxis by Cynthia Zarin

Lesson Eighteen – Wednesday

English – Alphabet Clothesline Review

Materials: String
                    Alphabet flash cards A-D
                    Snap clothespins

Preparation: Hang up the string to use as a clothesline.

Lesson:
1. Hang up the alphabet flash cards in random order.
2. Ask your child to try to put the letters in alphabetical order.
3. Sing the ABC song with them if they need help with this task.

Pre-Math – Number Scramble

Materials: Number flash cards (from lesson 7)

Preparation: None

Lesson:
1. Scramble the cards and see if your child can put them in order.
2. If they are really struggling with this task, try giving them only numbers 1 and 2 since those are the numbers you've been focusing on so far.
3. Then add in new numbers one at a time and have your child put them in order.

Art – Placemats

Materials: Construction paper
                    Black paint
                    Crayons or markers
                    Contact paper

Preparation: None

Lesson:
1. Let your child decorate their placemat with the crayons or markers.
2. Help your child to put paint on their hands and make hand prints on the construction paper.
3. Let the hand prints dry.
4. Cover their placemat with contact paper and let them use it for meals.

Gross Motor Skills – Sensory Bird Seed

Materials: Bird seed
                  Shovel or other sand toys
                  Large bucket or pan

Preparation: None

Lesson: Put the bird seed in the bucket and let your child play with it. You may want to do this activity outside.

Science – Animal Sort

Materials: Old magazines or newspaper inserts
                  Scissors

Preparation: Cut out a variety of different animal pictures. Be sure to include animals with black skin, fur or feathers.

Lesson:
1. Scatter the pictures in front of your child.
2. Ask them to sort out the animals by color.
3. Then, ask them to sort the animals into separate piles for those which have fur, feathers, or skin.

Literature -
Another pet by Trisha Speed Shaskan
The bath by Terri Dougherty
Before you were mine by Maribeth Boelts
The best pet of all by David LaRochelle

Lesson Nineteen – Thursday

English – Creative Drama

Materials: <u>Fables from Aesop</u> Adapted and Illustrated by
Tom Lynch (Tortoise & Hare)
Stuffed animal – turtle
Stuffed animal – rabbit
String

Preparation: Tie a string to the turtle and the rabbit.

Lesson:
1. Read the story of the "Tortoise and the Hare" to your child.
2. Allow them to act it out.
3. You might want to reread the story and have your child act it out while you're reading it. Or you might want to see how much of the story your child remembers by having them act out the story on their own.

Pre-Math – Dog Shapes Project

Materials: Construction paper
Scissors
Glue stick

Preparation:
1. Cut shapes out of the construction paper (medium circle for head; large circle for body; 7 ovals for ears, arms, legs and tail; 3 small circles for eyes and nose, one semi-circle for mouth).
2. Assemble an example project so that your child will know how to make their own dog.

Lesson:
1. Give your child the shapes that you have cut out.
2. Have them look at your example and determine how to use the cut out shapes to make their own dog.

Music – Follow the Leader

Materials: A drum (or a pan and a wooden spoon)

Preparation: None

Lesson:
1. Ask your child to repeat whatever rhythm you make on the drum.
2. Start with short rhythms and work your way up to longer rhythms.
3. After they have followed you correctly several times, turn them loose and let them play their drum at will. Or turn on some music and let them try to play the drum to the music.

Field Trip – Humane Society or Veterinarian's Office

Literature –
Fables from Aesop   Adapted and Illustrated by Tom Lynch   (read other fables)
Barn Cat by Carol P. Saul
Mr. Wishy Washy by Joy Cowley
Have You Seen My Cat? by Eric Carle

Lesson Twenty – Friday

English – Make an alligator

Materials: Long, rectangular box
Lots of egg carton cups (cut out individually)
Shorter box
Packing tape or masking tape
Glue
Green or brown paint

Preparation:
1. Round off one end of the short box.
2. Tape the two boxes end-to-end to become the form for your alligator body and head.

Lesson:
1. Give your child the alligator form and the egg carton cups.
2. Let him glue the cups (open side down) all over the boxes to represent the scaly skin.
3. Once the glue is dry, your child can paint their alligator.
4. Let your child decide what they'd like to use for eyes and legs.

Pre-Math – Find Two

Materials: Paper lunch bag
Two of several items (2 crayons, 2 cotton balls, 2 tiny blocks, 2 spoons, 2 rubber bands, etc.)

Preparation: Put the items in the lunch bag.

Lesson:
1. Have your child reach into the bag and try to remove two items which are the same without looking into the bag.
2. You may have to hold the bag over their head a bit if it is too tempting for your child to peek into the bag.

Art – Cat Paws

Materials: Card stock
                 Crayons
                 Black marker
                 Glue

Preparation: None

Lesson:
1. Using the black markers and the card stock, trace around your children's hands with their fingers bent inward to make cat paws.
2. If your child is able, let them cut out the paws (or you can help them if necessary).
3. Let your child color the one of the "paws" pink and one of them the color of cat fur (black, brown, gray, etc.)
4. Cut a strip of card stock (about 2" wide by 5" long) and have your child color it the same color as the rest of the cat fur. Measure your child's hands to determine the exact dimensions of the strip.
5. Make the strip into a ring and attach one paw to the top of the ring and one paw to the bottom.
6. Once it dries, your child can slip the ring over their hand and show the top and bottom of their cat paw.

Gross Motor Skills – Balance Beam

Materials: A 2x4 piece of lumber

Preparation: None

Lesson:
1. Lay the 2x4 down on the ground to use as a balance beam.
2. Try to have your child walk on balance beam forwards, backwards, and sideways without stepping off.
3. See if they can do it without looking at the board.
4. Encourage them to stick both arms out straight for balance.

Science – Creative Drama

Materials: None

Preparation: None

Lesson:
1. Let your child pretend to be a black cat.

Literature –
Zack's Alligator by Shirley Mozelle
Alligator alphabet by Stella Blackstone
The Pokey Little Puppy by Janette Sebring Lowrey
Millions of cats by Wanda Gág

Week Five

Your theme for this week will be *eating healthy foods*. You will be focusing on the following topics with your child:

English – The letter E
Pre-Math – Triangles and the number 3
Art – The color green

Lesson Twenty-One – Monday

English: Recognition of the Letter A

Materials: Card stock
                 Crushed eggshells
                 Glue

Preparation: Cut a capital letter E out of card stock.

Lesson: Let your child glue the crushed eggshells all over their capital E.

Pre-Math – Shape Matching

Materials: Shapes (from lesson 8)

Preparation: None

Lesson:
   1. Put the shapes on the floor in front of your child.
   2. Have your child match the shapes - first by size, then by color and finally by shape.

Art – Fringing

Materials: Construction paper
               Scissors

Preparation: Cut a large triangle out of the construction paper.

Lesson:
1. Give the triangle and the scissors to your child.
2. Have them fringe the entire outside of their triangle.

Fine Motor Skills – Bean Scoop

Materials: Bag of dried beans
               Spoon
               Two bowls

Preparation: None

Lesson:
1. Fill one bowl with the dried beans.
2. Give the spoon to your child.
3. Have your child scoop the beans from one bowl to the other.

Science – Spice Smell

Materials: A variety of spices (i.e., cinnamon, chili powder, garlic, nutmeg, etc.)

Preparation: None

Lesson:
1. Sit down with your child and talk to them about how we use different spices to make our food taste better.
2. Talk to them about how we try not to add salt to many things because it isn't healthy for us.
3. Open the spices one at a time and let your child smell them. Warn them in advance not to breathe too deeply of any strong spices.

Literature –
Please say please! : Penguin's guide to manners by Margery Cuyler
I want a blue banana! by Joyce and James Dunbar
Little Apple Goat by Caroline Jayne Church
Mr. Putter and Tabby pick the pears by Cynthia Rylant

Lesson Twenty-Two – Tuesday

English – Letter E

Materials: 4 Craft sticks
                Crayons
                Glue

Preparation: None

Lesson:
1. Give your child 4 craft sticks and let them color them. Encourage them to use the color green as that is the color we're focusing on this week.
2. Let your child glue the sticks together to form a Capital E.

Pre-Math – Vegetable Patterns

Materials: 3 Tomatoes
                3 Cucumbers
                3 Carrots

Preparation: None

Lesson:
1. On a table, help your child lay out the vegetables in a pattern. Begin with 2 veggies (i.e., alternate the tomatoes with the cucumbers.)
2. Ask your child to name the pattern.
3. Increase the difficulty by adding a third veggie (i.e., tomato, cucumber, carrot, tomato, cucumber, carrot, etc.)
4. Ask your child to name the pattern.
5. Let your child lay out a pattern for you to identify.

Lunch – Triangle Food

Materials: Sandwiches of your choice
                Triangle-shaped crackers or chips

Preparation: Make the sandwiches and cut them into triangle shapes (cut across both diagonally)

Lesson: Point out to your child that they are eating triangles for lunch.

Geography – State Map

Materials: State Map Outline
             Crayons

Preparation: Print out a map of your state. A great place to find these maps is on the
             internet at www.50states.com/maps/

Lesson:
1. Give the map of your state to your child.
2. Talk to them about where you live. Draw a star for them in that location.
3. Let your child color the map. Encourage them to use green or brown for the land
   and blue for any water.

Fine Motor Skills – Pack a Lunch

Materials: Paper lunch bag
             Old magazines or newspaper inserts
             Scissors

Preparation: None

Lesson:
1. Give your child a lunch bag and some old magazines.
2. Let them cut out foods they would like to have for their lunch and put them in
   their bag.
3. Once they have several foods in their bag, have them dump them out so you can
   discuss whether the items they picked are healthy foods or unhealthy foods.

Literature -
Strawberries are red by Petr Horácek
The ABC's of fruits and vegetables and beyond by Steve Charney & David Goldbeck
The fruit group by Mari C. Schuh
A fruit is a suitcase for seeds by Jean Richards

Lesson Twenty-Three – Wednesday

English – Memory Game

Materials: Fruit cutouts from companion download (or real fruit if you'd prefer)
A towel

Preparation:
1. Print copies of the fruits (see companion download.)
2. Cut out the fruits.
3. NOTE: No preparation necessary if using real fruit.

Lesson:
1. Lay the fruit down on the floor in front of your child.
2. Discuss the fruit. Help your child to identify their names, their colors, etc.
3. Put a towel over the fruit. Reach in and remove one fruit and don't let your child see which one.
4. Remove the towel and have your child try to guess which fruit is missing.

Pre-Math – Shapes Make Other Shapes

Materials: Triangle shapes (from lesson 8)

Preparation: None

Lesson:
1. Put two triangle shapes in front of your child.
2. See if they can figure out how to make a square using the triangles.
3. Put the rest of the triangle shapes in front of them and let them make more squares.

Fine Motor Skills – Marble Flick

Materials: Triangle (from lesson 8)
Marble

Preparation: None

Lesson: Let your child flick the marble onto the triangle, across the triangle, along the edges of the triangle, etc.

Art – Food Pyramid

Materials: Food Pyramid (from companion download)
                Old magazines or newspaper inserts
                Poster board or large construction paper
                Marker
                Ruler
                Glue Stick

Preparation:
1. Cut out pictures of different kinds of food from the old magazines.
2. Print the food pyramid from the companion download as an example.
3. Label the pyramid with the proper food groups.

Lesson:
1. Put the pictures in front of your child.
2. Let them sort through the pictures and glue them into the correct food groups
3. Save this food pyramid as you will be referring to it in a subsequent lesson.

Gross Motor Skills – Chair Maze

Materials: Chairs

Preparation: Place chairs around the room – some standing up, some lying down.

Lesson: Let your child crawl under the chairs, around the chairs, etc.

Science – Baby Food Taste Test

Materials: A variety of baby foods
                The equivalent foods in the adult variety

Preparation: Prepare the adult foods so that they're ready to be eaten.

Lesson:
1. Let your child try the baby food one at a time.
2. See if they can identify the food. Do they like it?
3. Let them try the adult variety of the food. Which one did they prefer?
4. Have them compare the taste and the texture of each.
5. Do the same things with the rest of the foods.

Literature -
Growing colors by Bruce McMillan
Vegetable soup : the nutritional ABC's by Dianne Warren and Susan Smith Jones
The wild bunch by Dee Lillegard
Alexander the Grape fruit and vegetable jokes compiled by Charles Keller

Lesson Twenty-Four – Thursday

English – Green Vegetable Color Comparisons

Materials: Can of peas
              Can of lima beans
              Can of green beans

Preparation: None

Lesson:
1. Open the cans.
2. Compare the various shades of green.
3. See if your child can find other items which are different shades of green.
4. Let your child sample one of each of the peas and beans. Ask them which one they prefer.

Pre-Math – Tri-Ominos

Materials: Tri-Ominos game

Preparation: None

Lesson:
1. Play Tri-Ominos with your child.
2. Have them say the name of the numbers while you're playing the game.

Music – I Love Colors

Materials: None

Preparation: None

Lesson: Sing the song and find green objects with your child.

I Love Colors
(To the Tune of "Three Blind Mice")

I love green. I love green.
Yes I do. Yes I do.
Please may I show a green thing to you
So you will love the green _____ too?   *(____ is the green object you want to point out to your child.)*
Have you ever seen such a sight in your life?
Oh, I love green. I love green.

Fine Motor Skills – Drawing Triangles

Materials: Paper
                 Crayons or pencil

Preparation: None

Lesson:
1. Let your child practice drawing triangles on their paper.
2. If your child struggles with this task, draw some triangles for them with yellow marker and let them begin by tracing them.
3. After they've completed tracing successfully, let them try to draw a few on their own.

Science – Eat a Flower Garden

Materials: A Variety of Vegetables
                 A plate

Preparation: Prepare vegetables to be used.

Lesson:
1. Let your child build a flower garden with vegetables.
    a. Round slices of cucumber or carrot can be flower blooms.
    b. Whole green beans, green pepper strips, carrot sticks, or celery sticks can be stems and tree trunks.
    c. Lettuce can be leaves or tree tops.
    d. Broccoli can be trees.
    e. Alfalfa sprouts can be grass.
    f. Rinsed kidney beans can be bugs.
2. Once it is completed, let your child eat their garden if they would like. If it turns out really cute, you might want to take a picture of it first.

Literature -
The Surprise Garden by Zoe Hall
A Child's Book of Manners by Ruth Shannon Odor
The Little Mouse, the Red, Ripe Strawberry, and the Big Hungry Bear by Don and
       Audrey Wood
Stone Soup by Ann McGovern

Lesson Twenty-Five – Friday

English – Let's Go Shopping

Materials: None

Preparation: None

Lesson:
1. Go to the grocery store with your child.
2. While there, say, "___ went to the grocery store and he/she bought something that begins with the letter E."
3. Do this at least for all letters that we've covered so far (A – E).
4. You can also do this for letters we haven't yet covered. As you pick up items, say the phrase for the correct letter and show the item to your child. Let them tell you what the item is. This will help them to begin recognizing the sounds of the different letters.

Pre-Math – Math Muffin Tins

Materials: Cupcake paper liners
               Marker
               Dried beans

Preparation: Write the numbers 1 – 10 on the muffin liners and put them in a row.

Lesson: Have your child count out the correct number of dried beans for each muffin liner and put them in.

Art – Fun With Green

Materials: Yellow construction paper
               Blue tissue paper

Preparation: None

Lesson:
1. Let your child cut out shapes from the blue tissue paper.
2. Let them glue the shapes onto the construction paper. They will see that the shapes become green.

Fine Motor Skills – Tasty Fingers

Materials: 10 different types of finger-tasting foods (i.e., Chocolate Sauce, Caramel, Whipped Cream, Different flavored Jellies, catsup, peanut butter, honey mustard, BBQ sauce, pudding, yogurt, etc.)
Paper plates
Glass of water

Preparation: Put dabs of 10 different items on each plate

Lesson:
1. Be sure your child washes his/her hands before this activity.
2. Have your child dip each finger of each hand into a different food (one at a time).
3. Let them drink a sip of water between foods to remove the former taste from their mouth.
4. This is a great fine motor activity as children must isolate each finger for dipping into the foods.

Science – Good and Bad Snacks

Materials: Oreos
Apple
Glass of water

Preparation: None

Lesson:
1. Give your child a couple of Oreos to eat.
2. After they've chewed them up, have them go look at their teeth in the mirror.
3. Have your child rinse out their mouth with water.
4. Now give them an apple to eat.
5. After they've chewed up several bites, have them go look at their teeth in the mirror again.
6. Talk to your child about how some foods are good for your teeth and others are not.

Literature -
Bread and Jam for Frances by Russell Hoban
Don't You Feel Well, Sam? by Amy Hest
A Mud Pie for Mother by Scott Beck
Mr. Putter and Tabby Pour the Tea by Cynthia Rylant

Week Six

Your theme for this week will be *Fall leaves*. You will be focusing on the following topics with your child:

English – The letter F
Pre-Math – Triangles and the number 3
Art – The color orange

Lesson Twenty-Six – Monday

English: Recognition of the Letter F

Materials: Card stock
               Glue
               Fallen leaves

Preparation: Cut a capital letter F out of card stock.

Lesson:
1. Go for a walk with your child. Collect fallen leaves from outside. You will use these leaves for several other activities this week as well – so be prepared to go for several walks – or collect a bunch!
2. Let your child glue the leaves onto their F.

Pre-Math – Match the Leaves

Materials: Fallen leaves

Preparation: None

Lesson:
1. Scatter some leaves in front of your child.
2. Have them sort the leaves in a variety of ways (i.e., by color, by type, by size, etc.)

Art – Timothy Triangle

Materials: Construction paper
                Crayons or markers
                Glue

Preparation:
1. Draw a triangle on the construction paper. Use a thick, black marker to make it easier for your child to be able to cut this out later.
2. Cut arms and legs and any other parts you'd like to out of the construction paper.

Lesson:
1. Let your child cut the triangle out of the construction paper.
2. Let them add the arms and legs to their triangle.
3. Help them to draw a face on Timothy Triangle and let them color him.

Fine Motor Skills – Fall Leaf Place Mats

Materials: Contact paper
                Fallen leaves
                Crayons (especially orange)
                A light-colored construction paper

Preparation: None

Lesson:
1. Tape several leaves to the table.
2. Place the construction paper over the cutouts (you may want to tape this down as well so that it doesn't move on your child)
3. Have your child rub several crayon colors over the leaves. (Note: To do rubbings, remove all of the paper from the crayon, lay the crayon down flat, and use it to rub over the object.)
4. Cover the front and back of the construction paper with contact paper and let your child use this as a placemat.

Science – Examine the Leaves

Materials: Fallen leaves
                Magnifying glass

Preparation: None

Lesson:
1. Let your child examine some leaves through a magnifying glass.
2. Show them how moving the magnifying glass closer and farther away will change the size of the image.

Literature -

Fall Leaves Fall! by Zoe Hall
A Tree is Nice by Janice May Udry
From Acorn to Oak Tree by Jan Kottke
How Does It Feel to Be a Tree? by Flo Morse

Lesson Twenty-Seven – Tuesday

English – Fall Colors Match

Materials: Markers (red, yellow, brown and orange)
               Index cards
               Fallen leaves (at least one red, one yellow, one brown and one orange)
               Basket or bowl

Preparation: On the index cards, write the names of the colors red, yellow, brown and orange with the matching marker color.

Lesson:
1. Put the leaves in the basket or bowl.
2. Hold up an index card with a color word on it.
3. Have your child dig through the basket and find all of the leaves which are that color.
4. Repeat for all of the colors.

Pre-Math – Shape Patterns

Materials: Shapes (from lesson 8)

Preparation: None

Lesson:
1. Make a shape pattern alternating two different shapes.
2. Ask your child to copy the pattern.
3. As your child is working, ask them the following:
   a. What are the names of the shapes?
   b. Which shape comes first?
   c. What pattern do you see?
   d. Ask your child to continue the pattern.

Art – Leaf Wreath

Materials: Fallen leaves
               Paper plate
               Glue

Preparation: Cut the center of the plate out.

Lesson: Let your child glue leaves onto the plate to form a wreath.

Gross Motor Skills – Blanket Riding

Materials: Blanket

Preparation: None

Lesson:
1. Have your child sit in the middle of the blanket.
2. Gently pull him/her around the room.

Literature -
Dot & Jabber and the Great Acorn Mystery by Ellen Stoll Walsh
Johnny Maple-Leaf by Alvin Tresselt
Fall is Here! I Love It! by Elaine W. Good
Deep In the Forest by Brinton Turkle

Lesson Twenty-Eight – Wednesday

English – Outlines

Materials: Black construction paper
White chalk
Orange Fruit Loops
Glue

Preparation:
1. Separate out the orange Fruit Loops from the box.
2. Using the chalk, write a big bubble three on the construction paper.

Lesson:
1. Give your child the construction paper and the glue. Have them trace the outer edges of the 3 with the glue.
2. Let them place the orange Fruit Loops along the outer edges of the 3 (on top of the glue.)

Pre-Math – Mixed Nuts Sorting

Materials: A jar of mixed nuts

Preparation: None

Lesson:
1. Dump out a pile of mixed nuts in front of your child.
2. Let them sort the nuts into different piles.

Geography – Country Map

Materials: Outline map of the United States (or the country in which you live)
Crayons

Preparation: Print a copy of your country's map. You can get great maps from
www.worldatlas.com/webimage/testmaps/maps.htm

Lesson:
1. Give the map of your country to your child.
2. Talk to them about where you live. Draw a star for them in that location.
3. Let your child color the map. Encourage them to use green or brown for the land and blue for any water.

Gross Motor Skills – Walk on a Triangle

Materials: Masking tape

Preparation: Make a large triangle out of masking tape on the floor.

Lesson:
1. March around the triangle with your child – try to get them to keep their feet on top of the tape as much as possible.
2. While marching, say "Marching on the Triangle" over and over to help your child remember what shape they're marching on.
3. You can put on music to have your child march to that as well, if you would like.

Science – Make an Owl

Materials: 2 Leaves
               Construction paper
               2 buttons
               Crayons
               Glue

Preparation: Cut an oval out of the construction paper.

Lessons:
1. Give your child the oval and leaves. Let them glue the leaves onto the oval to make wings.
2. Glue the buttons on the oval to make eyes.
3. Let your child color their owl.

Literature -
Miss Nelson is Missing! by James Marshall
All By Myself by Mercer Mayer
When Will it Snow? by Bruce Hiscock
Good-Night, Owl! by Pat Hutchins

Lesson Twenty-Nine – Thursday

English: Further Recognition of the Letter F

Materials: Card stock
                    Glue
                    Feathers (from dollar store feather duster)

Preparation: Cut a capital letter F out of card stock.

Lesson: Let your child glue the leaves onto their F.

Pre-Math – Mixed Nuts Counting and Patterning

Materials: Jar of mixed nuts

Preparation: None

Lesson:
1. Put a handful of nuts in front of your child.
2. Have them count out different amounts of nuts.
3. Make a pattern with the nuts. (start out alternating two nuts and slowly add additional nuts to your patterns)
4. Have your child copy the patterns.

Music – Follow the Leader

Materials: None

Preparation: None

Lesson:
1. Sit down on the floor with your child.
2. Clap out different rhythms and have your child try to copy the rhythm.
3. Sing different phrases and have them copy you.
4. Stomp different rhythms and have them copy you, etc.

Fine Motor Skills – Magic Mud

Materials: Cornstarch (or can use Jello, pudding, whipped cream, yogurt, etc.)
A bowl
Water
Food Coloring

Preparation:
1. Put a box of cornstarch in the bowl.
2. Add just enough water to be able to stir the mixture.
3. Stir in food coloring.

Lesson:
1. Let your child play with the mixture with their fingers.
2. Another option for this activity, if you're brave, is to let your child step in this mixture with bare feet! ☺

Literature -
Blueberries for Sal by Robert McCloskey
Mouse's First Fall by Lauren Thompson
Fall is Here: Counting 1 to 10 by Pamela Jane
Fletcher and the Falling Leaves by Julia Rawlinson

Lesson Thirty – Friday

English – Nature Journal

Materials: Paper or notebook
                  Crayons or colored pencils
                  Bag

Preparation: None

Lesson:
1. Go for a walk in the woods with your child.
2. Observe nature with your child. Tell them to watch for animals or other things about which they might like to write a story.
3. Collect some leaves for later activities.
4. Once back home, have your child draw a picture of something they observed. You should also draw a picture so that your child has an idea of what you're expecting them to do.
5. Let your child dictate a story of the something they observed – or of your entire nature walk. Write down their story word-for-word on their paper.

Pre-Math – Counting Candy

Materials: Reeses Pieces or M&Ms
                  Paper plate

Preparation: None

Lesson:
1. Put a handful of the candy on your child's plate.
2. Let them count the candy and sort the candy by color.
3. Help them to create sets of 3.
4. Let them eat the candy.

Art – Leafy People

Materials: Various sizes of leaves
                Glue
                Construction paper
                Crayons or markers

Preparation: None

Lesson:
1. Tell your child to make a picture of their family using the leaves. They can use the leaves for the bodies, for clothing, or for anything else they would like.
2. You may want to suggest to your child that they make stick figures of each family member before they start gluing on leaves… but leave that decision up to them.

Gross Motor Skills – Raking

Materials: Small rake

Preparation: None

Lesson: Go outside with your child and rake leaves with them. This is wonderful for their gross motor skills.

Science – Nutty Painting

Materials: A variety of nuts
                A shoebox lid
                Orange paint
                Construction paper

Preparation: Cut the construction paper so that it will fit inside the box lid.

Lesson:
1. Let your child dip a few nuts into the paint.
2. Have them place them on the paper and then move the box lid around forcing the nuts to move around.
3. This will create a painting.

Literature –
Reese's Pieces peanut butter candy in a crunchy shell : counting board book by Jerry
        Pallotta
In the Leaves by Huy Voun Lee
Fall Leaves by Grace Maccarone
Fall Leaf Project by Margaret McNamara

Week Seven

Your theme for this week will be the *grocery store*. You will be focusing on the following topics with your child:

English – The letter G
Pre-Math – Rectangles and the number 4
Art – The color yellow

Lesson Thirty-One – Monday

English: Recognition of the Letter G

Materials: Card stock
              Paper grocery bag
              Glue stick

Preparation: Cut a capital letter G out of card stock.

Lesson: Let your child rip pieces off of the grocery bag and glue them onto their
              capital letter G.

Pre-Math – Grocery Store Play

Materials: Empty boxes and cans
                Paper
                Black construction paper
                Tape
                Markers
                Grocery Bags

Preparation:
1. Label the boxes and cans with price tags (using the numbers 1 – 10.)
2. Put boxes and cans on a bookshelf to resemble a grocery store.
3. Tape the black construction paper in a loop around a small table to be the check-out conveyer belt.

Lesson:
1. Give your child the grocery bags. Let them do some shopping.
2. You can direct your child's play by asking them to get all of the items which cost 2 cents, all of the items with yellow on them, etc.
3. You can also work with your child to help them count the items when they get to the "checkout lane."

Art – Field Trip to Grocery Store

Materials: Paper
                Crayons or colored pencils

Preparation: None

Lesson:
1. Go to the grocery store with your child.
2. Tell your child to watch for people or other things about which they might like to write a story.
3. Once back home, have your child draw a picture of something they observed. You should also draw a picture so that your child has an idea of what you're expecting them to do.
4. Let your child dictate a story of something they observed – or of your entire trip to the grocery store.

Gross Motor Skills – Hot Potato

Materials: Medium-sized ball

Preparation: None

Lesson:
1. Sit on the ground with your child.
2. Use your feet to push the "hot potato" (ball) back and forth between the two of you.
3. Try to keep control of the ball and not have it fly around wildly. You may want to play this game outdoors.

Science – The Sound and Taste of G

Materials: Gingerbread Baby by Jan Brett
                Gingerbread man cookies (homemade or store bought)
                Green frosting
                Sprinkles
                Plastic knife or cheese spreader

Preparation: None

Lesson:
1. Talk to your child about the two sounds that G makes (as in "green" and "gingerbread").
2. Read the book Gingerbread Baby by Jan Brett.
3. If using homemade cookies, go ahead and make them with your child at this time. Let your child do as much of it (with your assistance) as possible.
4. After the cookies cool, let your child frost the cookies and put sprinkles on them.
5. Eat some cookies.

Literature -
The supermarket mice by Margaret Gordon
Adventures of Cow as told to Lori Korchek
Max goes to the grocery store by Adria F. Klein
My favorite foods by Dana Meachen Rau

Lesson Thirty-Two – Tuesday

English - Hola Jalapeño!

Materials: Hola Jalapeño! by Amy Wilson Sanger
                       Ingredients to make tacos
                       Index Card
                       Marker

Preparation: Write down step-by-step instructions on how to make tacos on the index card.

Lesson:
1. Read the book Hola Jalapeño! by Amy Wilson Sanger.
2. Make tacos with your child. Follow the recipe you wrote down earlier. Be sure to point out the steps and the words to your child.
3. Eat the tacos.

Pre-Math – Coupon Count

Materials: Coupon sections from newspaper
                       Scissors

Preparation: None

Lesson:
1. Cut out coupons with your child.
2. Let them choose which foods they might like to try.
3. Talk to them about how some of these foods are healthy and some aren't so healthy.
4. Let your child find coupons that have the number 4 in them.

Geography – Maps of Continents

Materials: Outline map of the Continents (see companion
               download)
               Crayons

Preparation: Print a map of the continents.

Lesson:
1. Give the map of the continents to your child.
2. Label the continents.
4. Talk to them about where you live. Draw a star for them in that location.
5. Let your child color the land on the map. Encourage them to use green or brown for the land.
6. Leave the oceans blank and save the map. You will be coloring them in during a subsequent lesson.

Fine Motor Skills – Drawing Rectangles

Materials: Paper
               Crayons or pencil

Preparation: None

Lesson:
1. Have your child practice drawing rectangles on their paper.
2. If your child struggles with this, draw some rectangles for them with yellow marker and let them trace them. After they've completed this task, let them practice drawing some rectangles on their own.

Literature –
The Yellow Balloon by Charlotte Dematons
Shopping for lunch by Susan Blackaby
Where are you? by Francesca Simon
The supermarket by B.A. Hoena

Lesson Thirty-Three – Wednesday

English – Additional Recognition of the Letter G

Materials: Card stock
                    Glitter
                    Glue

Preparation: Cut out a large capital G from the card stock.

1. Have your child trace the outside edges of the G with the glue.
2. Over a garbage can, help your child shake glitter onto the glue. Then help them to dump off the excess glitter into the garbage can.

Pre-Math – Number Hunt

Materials: Grocery store ads from newspaper
                    Markers

Preparation: None

Lesson:
1. Give your child a page from the grocery store ads.
2. Call out different numbers (1 – 4) and let your child circle those numbers in their ad.

Art – Four Part Collage

Materials: Old magazines or newspaper inserts
                    Scissors
                    Glue stick
                    Construction paper

Preparation: None

Lesson:
1. Have your child look for pictures that have four parts. Also have them look for the number 4.
2. Have them cut out these pictures and glue them to their construction paper to make a collage.

Fine Motor Skills – Geoboard Play

Materials: Geoboard

Preparation: None

Lesson:
1. Let your child play with the geoboard.
2. Show them how they can make all sorts of different shapes with the rubber bands.
3. Concentrate on making rectangles since that is the shape we're focusing on this week.

Science – Rectangle Snack

Materials: Graham crackers
                Peanut butter
                Plastic knife or cheese spreader

Preparation: None

Lesson:
1. Discuss and feel the graham cracker's rectangular shape.
2. Have your child break their cracker into smaller rectangles.
3. Have your child spread peanut butter on their cracker to make rectangle sandwiches.

Literature -
Don't forget the bacon! by Pat Hutchins
Five little monkeys go shopping by Eileen Christelow
The Good-Day Bunnies shopping day by Harriet Margolin and Carol Nicklaus
Harry hates shopping! by Ronda and David Armitage

Lesson Thirty-Four – Thursday

English – Food Journal

Materials: Construction paper
                     Crayons or colored pencils
                     Food pyramid (created in Lesson 22)

Preparation: None

Lesson:
1. Review the completed food pyramid.
2. Show your child how you will be recording everything that they eat that day in the proper category.
3. Let your child draw pictures to accompany the words you write for what they eat.
4. At the end of the day, show your child how well they did at having a balanced and healthy diet that day.

Pre-Math – Fraction Puzzles

Materials: Construction paper (5 different colors)
                     Scissors
                     Markers

Preparation: None

Lesson:
1. Show your child a piece of construction paper. Show them how it is a whole piece. Write WHOLE on the piece.
2. Cut one color of the construction paper in half. Write ½ on each piece.
3. Cut another color of the construction paper into thirds. Write 1/3 on each piece.
4. Cut another color of the construction paper into fourths. Write ¼ on each piece.
5. Cut another color of the construction paper into eighths. Write 1/8 on each piece.
6. Let your child put the pieces back together. Start by laying the whole piece on the table. Then have your child reassemble the other layers of construction paper by laying them on top of the whole piece, one by one.

Music – Feel the Beat

Materials: CD with Classical Music of your Choice

Preparation: None

Lesson:
1. Dance with your child to the music.
2. Tell them to dance fast when the music is fast and slowly when it's slow.

Fine Motor Skills – Play-Doh

Materials: Play Doh
               Rolling Pin, plastic knife, cookie cutters, etc.

Preparation: None

Lesson:
   1. Let your child play with the Play-Doh.
   2. You can have them make a snake and bend it around to form the letter G.

Literature -
I'm so mad! by Robie Harris
Jonathan goes to the grocery store by Susan K. Baggette
Just shopping with mom by Mercer Mayer
Maisy goes shopping by Lucy Cousins

Lesson Thirty-Five – Friday

English – G is for Grapes

Materials: G is for Grapes Worksheet (see companion download)

Preparation: Print the worksheet from the companion download.

Lesson: Let your child color the worksheet.

Pre-Math – Counting Grapes

Materials: Bunch of grapes

Preparation: None

Lesson:
1. Ask your child to put grapes in groups of 1, 2, 3, and 4.
2. Let your child eat the grapes.

Art – Rhonda Rectangle

Materials: Construction paper
               Crayons or markers
               Scissors
               Glue

Preparation:
1. Draw a rectangle on the construction paper. Use a thick, black marker to make it easier for your child to be able to cut this out later.
2. Cut arms and legs and any other parts you'd like to out of the construction paper.

Lesson:
1. Let your child cut the rectangle out of the construction paper.
2. Let them add the arms and legs to their rectangle.
3. Help them to draw a face on Rhonda Rectangle and let them color her.

Fine Motor Skills – Grab the Grapes

Materials: Grapes
               Tongs
               Two bowls

Preparation: Put the grapes individually into one of the bowls.

Lesson: Have your child move the grapes from one bowl to the other using the tongs.

Literature -
<u>Mama, Papa, and Baby Joe</u> by Niki Daly
<u>Mrs. Pirate</u> by Nick Sharrat
<u>On Market Street</u> by Arnold Lobel
<u>Shopping with Samantha</u> by Teddy Slater

Week Eight

Your theme for this week will be *Helping Others and Community Helpers*. You will be focusing on the following topics with your child:

English – The letter H
Pre-Math – Rectangles and the number 4
Art – The color purple

Lesson Thirty-Six – Monday

English: Recognition of the Letter H

Materials: Card stock
                Hay
                Glue

Preparation: Cut a capital letter H out of card stock.

Lesson: Let your child glue the hay to their H.

Pre-Math – Fabric Shapes

Materials: Fabric scraps
                Scissors

Preparation: None

Lesson: Let your child cut some basic shapes from the fabric. Be sure they cut some rectangles since that is the shape we are focusing on this week.

Art – Helping Hand

Materials: Construction paper
               Markers
               Crayons

Preparation: None

Lesson:
1. With the markers and the construction paper, trace your child's hand with their fingers wide open.
2. Have your child tell you five things they can do to help around the house this week.
3. Write these things down for them inside the fingers and thumb of their hand.
4. Hang up their Helping Hand on the refrigerator. When your child helps with each activity, let them color in that finger.

Gross Motor Skills – Zig Zag Run

Materials: Masking tape

Preparation: Make a zig zag line on the floor with the masking tape.

Lesson:
1. Let your child walk and run back and forth on the zig zag line.
2. Try to have them keep their feet as close to the line as possible.

Literature –
Alphabet rescue by Audrey Wood
The Wheels on the Bus by Paul O. Zelinsky
Papa, Please Get the Moon for Me by Eric Carle
Caps for Sale by Esphyr Slobodkina

Lesson Thirty-Seven – Tuesday

English – Be a Helper

Materials: None

Preparation: None

Lesson:
1. Give your child examples of situations they might encounter and have them try to tell you what they should do to help.
    a. Your little sister spilled her milk on the floor. What should you do?
    b. Your friend is cutting up paper with scissors and there is quite a mess all over the table. Mommy says it is time to clean up. What should you do?
    c. Your grandma dropped her book when she walked into the room. What should you do?
    d. Your brother is trying to get his bike out of the garage – but the door keeps shutting on him. What should you do?
    e. Your friend was putting their puzzle away when they accidentally dropped it and it fell all over the floor. What should you do?
    f. Your daddy can't seem to find his glasses. What should you do?

Pre-Math – Purple Patterns

Materials: Purple construction paper
               Yellow construction paper

Preparation: Cut out several rectangles from both colors of construction paper.

Lesson:
1. Make a pattern with the purple and yellow rectangles.
2. Ask your child to copy the pattern.
5. As your child is working, ask them the following:
    a. What are the names of the shapes?
    b. Which color shape comes first?
    c. What pattern do you see?
    d. Ask your child to continue the pattern.

Geography – Oceans of the World

Materials: Map from lesson 31
                Crayons

Preparation: None

Lesson:
1. Give the map of the world to your child.
2. Label the oceans.
3. Talk to them about which oceans are the closest to where they live.
4. Let your child color oceans on the map. Encourage them to use blue for the water.

Gross Motor Skills – Litter Toss

Materials: Garbage can
                Newspaper

Preparation: None

Lesson:
1. Discuss litter with your child.
2. Have them wad up sheets of newspaper and throw it on the ground.
3. Then have them pick up the pieces of litter one at a time. Have them try to toss the litter from wherever they're at into the garbage can.

Literature –
Just Like Mama by Beverly Lewis
Five Silly Fishermen by Roberta Edwards
The Class Trip by Grace Maccarone
A Color of His Own by Leo Lionni

Lesson Thirty-Eight – Wednesday

English – Be the Doctor

Materials: Ace wrap bandages
                Any other braces or slings you have at home

Preparation: None

Lesson:
1. Pretend you are sick and let your child pretend to be the doctor.
2. Let them wrap you up with ace wrap, put braces on your arm, etc.
3. Then let your child take a turn being sick and you can be the doctor.
4. Try to talk like a real doctor so that your child becomes familiar with the language that a doctor would typically use with a patient.

Pre-Math – Counting Corn

Materials: Egg carton
                Dried corn kernels
                Marker

Preparation: Cut out a 4-cup section from the egg carton. Label the sections 1 – 4.

Lesson:
1. Give your child a handful of corn.
2. Have them count the corn and put the correct amount in each section of the egg carton.
3. Be sure to give your child more corn than they need so that they will have to count the corn for each section.

Art – Ouchie Art

Materials: A variety of band-aids
                Construction paper
                Crayons or markers

Preparation: None

Lesson:
1. Give your child a stack of band-aids and the construction paper.
2. Let them stick the band-aids to the paper, making a design of their choice.
3. They can color their paper once they've stuck several band-aids to it.

Fine Motor Skills – Grab the Gauze

Materials: Several squares of gauze
                  Tweezers
                  2 bowls

Preparation: Put the gauze into one of the bowls.

Lesson: Have your child use the tweezers to transfer the gauze from one bowl to the other.

Literature -
Barn Raising by Craig Brown
The Little Engine That Could by Watty Piper
Doctor DeSoto by William Steig
Keep the Lights Burning, Abbie by Peter and Connie Roop

Lesson Thirty-Nine – Thursday

English – Name the Helper

Materials: Pictures of Community Helpers Hats (see companion download)

Preparation: Print the community helpers hats from the companion download. Cut them out so they're on individual squares.

Lesson: Hold up the hat pictures one at a time and have your child try to identify which kind of community helper would wear it.

Pre-Math – House of Shapes

Materials: Piece of bread (house)
Triangular piece of cheese (roof)
Slices of carrot (windows)
Small, rectangular-shaped cracker (door)
Plate

Preparation: None

Lesson:
1. Put the food on your child's plate.
2. Tell them to make a house with it. See what they come up with on their own. You can help them out if they get stuck.
3. Let your child eat their house.

Music – Rectangle Marching

Materials: Masking tape

Preparation: Make a large rectangle on the floor with the masking tape.

Lesson:
1. Let your child march on the rectangle.
2. While marching, chant the following with your child:
   a. "We're marching on the rectangle…"
   b. "We're marching on a long side…"
   c. "We're marching on a short side…"

Fine Motor Skills – Stacking Blocks

Materials: Four rectangle-shaped blocks

Preparation: None

Lesson: Have your child see how many different ways they can stack the blocks.

Literature –
The Construction Alphabet Book by Jerry Pallotta
Officer Buckle and Gloria by Peggy Rathmann
My Doctor by Harlow Rockwell
Clifford's Good Deeds by Norman Bridwell

Lesson Forty – Friday

English – Monkeys Jumping on the Bed

Materials: Five Little Monkeys Jumping on the Bed by Eileen
Christelow

Preparation: None

Lesson:
1. Read the book Five Little Monkeys Jumping on the Bed by Eileen Christelow
2. Do the rhyme with your child: *(hold up the appropriate number of fingers at the start of each verse)*

Five Little Monkeys
Five little monkeys jumping on the bed
One fell off and bumped his head
Mama called the doctor and the doctor said,
"No more monkeys jumping on the bed!"

Four little monkeys jumping on the bed…

Three little monkeys jumping on the bed…

(and so on).

Pre-Math – Purple Collage

Materials: Old magazines or newspaper inserts
Scissors
Glue stick
Construction paper

Preparation: None

Lesson:
1. Have your child look through the old magazines. Ask them to cut out pictures of things which have purple on them.
2. Have your child glue these items onto their construction paper to make a purple collage.

Art – Doctor's Appointment Journal

Materials: Paper or notebook
               Crayons or colored pencils

Preparation: None

Lesson:
1. Talk to your child about their last doctor's appointment. See what they can remember on their own, or what they can remember after you prompt them a bit.
2. Have your child draw a picture of something that happened during their last appointment.
3. Let your child dictate a story to you as well. Write down the story word-for-word on their paper.

Gross Motor Skills – Four Feathers

Materials: Four feathers (from a dollar store feather duster)

Preparation: None

Lesson:
1. Give your child the feathers to do with as he or she pleases.
2. You can make these suggestions:
   a. blow them up in the air
   b. blow them off a table
   c. toss them up and try to catch
   d. sandbox play
   e. throw them up in a breeze
   f. throw them up in front of a fan, etc.

Science – Scales for Mail

Materials: Paper
                     Crayons or colored pencils
                     A stamp
                     Boxes of different weights
                     A bathroom scale

Preparation:
1. Fill up some boxes so that they weight different amounts.
2. Label the boxes with fake addresses – be sure to use different zip codes.
3. Make signs with zip codes that correspond to the zip codes you used on the boxes. Hang these signs up on the walls around the house.

Lesson:
1. Show your child the stamp. Study the stamp with them a bit, pointing out the cost of each stamp in the corner.
2. Let your child draw some stamps of their own. Help them cut them out.
3. Set up a mini-post office with the boxes, the scale, and the stamps they just created.
4. Let your child weigh the boxes and attach whatever amount of postage they feel might be correct.
5. Explain to your child that delivering mail is like a big matching game. Help your child deliver the boxes to the proper zip code (using the signs that are hung up on the walls.)

Literature –
Postal Workers by Paulette Bourgeois
The Night Pirates by Peter Harris
At the Firehouse by Anne Rockwell
Horton Hatches the Egg by Dr. Seuss

Week Nine

Your theme for this week will be *Indians and Pilgrims*. You will be focusing on the following topics with your child:

English – The letter I
Pre-Math – Diamonds and the number 5
Art – The color brown

Lesson Forty-One– Monday

English: Recognition of the Letter I

Materials: Card stock
              Ice cube
              Food coloring (yellow, blue & red)
              Wash cloth
              Newspaper
              Bowl
              Paint smock or an old shirt

Preparation: Cut a capital letter I out of card stock.

Lesson:
1. Have your child put on their paint smock or an old shirt to protect their clothing. Have them roll up the sleeves to minimize the mess.
2. Put some water in a bowl which is wide enough to easily accommodate your child's fist. Spread the newspapers out to protect your work surface.
3. Add some yellow, blue and red food coloring to the water and mix it up.
4. Let your child hold onto the ice cube with the washcloth. Have them dip the ice cube into the colored water and paint their I with it.

Pre-Math – Turkey Feather Counting

Materials: Brown felt
               Orange or yellow felt
               Outline of a turkey (see companion download)
               Outline of a feather (see companion download)
               Black marker

Preparation:
1. Print the outlines of a turkey and a feather from the companion download to use as templates.
2. Cut out five turkeys from the felt.
3. Cut out 17 feathers from a different colored felt.
4. Write the numbers 1 – 5 on the bodies of the turkeys.
5. You can decorate the turkeys to look more like turkeys if you would like.

Lesson:
1. Give your child the turkeys and the feathers.
2. Have them place the correct number of feathers on each turkey.
3. (optional) You can let your child glue their turkeys and their feathers onto construction paper if you would like. Otherwise, you can keep the turkeys handy and let your child do them again throughout the week.

History – The Pilgrims

Materials: Pilgrim Cat by Carol Antoinette Peacock
               Empty paper towel roll
               Markers

Preparation: None

Lesson:
1. Read the book Pilgrim Cat.
2. Let your child make a telescope from the paper towel roll. Let them decorate it with markers.
3. Role play with your child that you're on the Mayflower. Encourage them to think about how happy they would have been once they finally saw land through the telescope.

Art – Leaf Turkey

Materials: Fallen leaves
                     Turkey outline (see companion download)
                     Crayons or markers
                     Glue

Preparation: Print the turkey outline on a piece of paper.

Lesson:
1. Give your child their art supplies.
2. Have them color their turkey body and decorate it.
3. Help them to glue their leaves onto the construction paper in a fan-shape.
4. Help them to glue the turkey body onto such a way that the leaves behind it look like feathers.
5. Let your child draw legs and feet and decorate their picture however they would like.

Gross Motor Skills – Turkey Toss Game

Materials: Paper grocery bag
                     2 brown lunch bags
                     Glue
                     Sock balls or bean bags

Preparation: Gather the small lunch bags at the tops. Then glue them to the sides of the grocery bag to look like drumsticks.

Lesson: You and your child take turns tossing the socks balls or bean bags into the "turkey".

Science – Turkey Feathers

Materials: A variety of bird feathers
                     Magnifying glass

Preparation: None – unless you want to take a walk outside with your child to search for feathers.

Lesson:
1. Let your child examine the different bird feathers with the magnifying glass.
2. Be sure to have them wash their hands thoroughly when they're done with this lesson.

Literature –
Thanksgiving Day Alphabet by Beverly Barras Vidrine
Priscilla Alden and the First Thanksgiving by Alice Benjamin Boynton
The amazing turkey rescue by Steve Metzger
Beauty and the beaks : a turkey's cautionary tale by Mary Jane and Herm Auch

Lesson Forty-Two – Tuesday

English – Native American Symbols

Materials: Brown construction paper
               Crayons or markers
               Native American symbols (see companion download or look up more on
               the Internet)

Preparation: Cut the brown construction paper to look like an animal hide. Print a copy
               of the Native American symbols from the companion download.

Lesson: Let your child tell a story using Native American Symbols – or just let
               them attempt to copy a few of the symbols on their "animal hide".

Pre-Math – How Many Fingers?

Materials: Card stock
               Scissors

Preparation: Cut hands out of the card stock with different numbers of fingers sticking
               up (1 – 5.)

Lesson:
1. Have your child count their fingers by touching them one at a time and saying the
   number.
2. Then give them the card stock hands one at a time.
3. Ask your child to count the number of fingers that is sticking up on the hand they
   are holding.
4. Repeat this process until your child has counted the fingers on all of the hands.

History – Pilgrim Hat

Materials: (for a boy)
10x13" Black construction paper
9x12" Gray construction paper
Tape
Pen or pencil
Scissors
Glue

(for a girl)
12 by 18 inch white construction paper
Glue
Scissors
Hole punch
Yarn

Preparation: None

Lesson: Instructions for assembling the hats are in the companion download, as they are different for boys and girls.

Geography – Plymouth Rock

Materials: Map created in lessons 31 and 36

Preparation: None

Lesson: Help your child to trace the route of the Pilgrims – from England to Cape Cod, Massachusetts.

Fine Motor Skills – Draw the Line

Materials: Paper
Crayons or pencil

Preparation: None

Lesson: Have your child practice drawing vertical lines on a piece of paper.

Literature -
Indian Two Feet and the ABC Moose Hunt by Margaret Friskey
The boy who loved morning by Shannon K. Jacobs
The courage of Sarah Noble by Alice Dalgliesh
David's little Indian : a story by Margaret Wise Brown

Lesson Forty-Three – Wednesday

English – Native American Book

Materials: Construction paper
Old magazines (National Geographic works well)
Glue stick
Markers
Stapler

Preparation: None

Lesson:
1. Ask your child to cut out various pictures of Native Americans from the magazines.
2. Use the construction paper to make a book.
3. Let your child glue their pictures onto the pages.
4. Have your child dictate the narration for each page and you can write it down for them.
5. Staple the book together.
6. Be sure to write your child's name on the front cover of the book with yellow highlighter and let them trace it.

Pre-Math – Tally Marks

Materials: Pencil
Paper

Preparation: None

Lesson: Show your child how to make tally marks for the numbers 1 – 5. Let them practice on their paper.

Art – Turkey Feathers

Materials: Feathers (from dollar store feather duster)
                       Turkey outline (see companion download)
                       Construction paper
                       Glue

Preparation:
1. Print the turkey outline from the companion download.
2. Either cut the turkey out for your child or let them cut it out, depending on their ability.

Lesson:
1. Help your child to glue their feathers onto the construction paper in a fan shape.
2. Let your child color their turkey and decorate him as much as they would like.
3. Have your child glue their turkey body on top of the feathers.

Gross Motor Skills – Turkey Bowling

Materials: Five empty 2-liter pop bottles
                       Sand (optional)
                       Brown spray paint
                       Feathers (from dollar store feather duster)
                       Ball

Preparation:
1. Make the pop bottles look like turkeys by spray painting them brown and gluing on the feathers.
2. You can fill the bottles half full with sand if you would like them to be a bit more stable. It will work just fine to leave them empty as well if you don't want to deal with the mess.

Lesson:
1. Set up the "turkeys" as you would bowling pins.
2. Have your child roll the ball toward the turkeys and see how many he/she can knock over.

English – Native American Story

Materials: Turtle's Race with Beaver. color illustrations by Jose Aruego and Ariane Dewey

Preparation: None

Lesson: Read this traditional Seneca story to your child and discuss the moral.

Science – The Smells of Thanksgiving

Materials: Construction paper
              Scissors
              Glue
              5 Spices (pepper, sage, pumpkin pie spice, cinnamon, nutmeg, etc.)
              Marker

Preparation: None

Lesson:
1. Write "The Smells of Thanksgiving" on the bottom of the construction paper.
2. Trace around your child's hand on the construction paper. Make sure their fingers are spread wide apart.
3. Let your child spread glue on each of their paper fingers.
4. Hold your child's paper over a garbage can and have them sprinkle one spice on each finger.
5. Help them to shake off the excess spices into the garbage can.
6. Let your child smell the spices as they put them on the paper. Ask them which spice they like the best.

Literature:
Sometimes it's Turkey - Sometimes it's Feathers by Lorna Balian
Over the River and Through the Wood by Lydia Maria Child
10 fat turkeys by Tony Johnston
Albuquerque turkey by B.G. Ford

Lesson Forty-Four – Thursday

English – Corn Husk Doll

Materials: Corn husks from 1-2 ears of corn
                  String

Preparation:
1. Cut the cob, remove the husks and save the corn silk.
2. Dry everything in the sun for 1-3 days.
3. Soak corn husks in warm water for 10 minutes.
4. Cut the thin ends off.

Lesson:
1. Bundle the thin end of 6 leaves around the corn silk ("hair.") Put the shiny side of the leaves toward the inside. Tie tightly with string.
2. Peal the leaves down and around to form the head. Hair should sprout up in the middle at this point.
3. Tie the neck area tightly with string.
4. Braid 3 strips of a leaf into a 6" piece for the arms.
5. Braid 2 more lengths in the same way to use later for the legs.
6. Put the arms under the neck (perpendicular to the other leaves.) Insert a rolled leaf under the arms to fill out and form the body.
7. Tie the waist area with string.
8. Insert the legs and secure them by tying 2 of the leaves which are forming the body from front to back. Trim the excess below the waist.
9. Wrap and tie one or two strips around top of legs to form hips.

Pre-Math – Shapes Skills

Materials: Shapes created in lesson 8

Preparation: None

Lesson:
1. Give your child various colors and sizes of circles, squares, triangles, rectangles and diamonds.
2. Have them sort the shapes into separate piles.
3. Really concentrate on the diamond as that is the shape for this week. Talk with your child about this shape and help them to learn its name.

Geography – Plymouth Rock

Materials: Squanto and the First Thanksgiving by Teresa Celsi

Preparation: None

Lesson:
1. Read the book Squanto and the First Thanksgiving by Teresa Celsi.
2. Role play being on the Mayflower and finally landing at Plymouth Rock. Role play whatever other scenes from the book your child would like to act out as well.

Art – Apple Turkeys

Materials: Apple
               Pretzel sticks
               Mini marshmallows
               Large marshmallow
               Toothpicks

Preparation: None

Lesson:
1. Help your child to poke holes in their apple with a toothpick.
2. Have your child poke several pretzel sticks into one side of their apple – then fill the pretzels up with mini marshmallows to make the tail feathers.
3. Have them poke a pretzel into the opposite side of the apple for its neck – then put a large marshmallow on it to be the turkey's head.
4. Your child can poke broken bits of pretzel sticks into the large marshmallow to be the eyes and the beak.
5. Let your child eat their apple turkey.

Fine Motor Skills – Diamond Punch

Materials: Construction paper
               Hole punch

Preparation: Cut a large diamond shape out of the construction paper.

Lesson:
1. Give your child their diamond and the hole punch.
2. Ask them to punch holes along all four edges of the diamond.

Literature –
Squanto and the First Thanksgiving by Teresa Celsi
Friendship's First Thanksgiving by William Accorsi
The great turkey race by Steve Metzger
One tough turkey : a Thanksgiving story by Steven Kroll

Lesson Forty-Five – Friday

English – My Indian Name

Materials: The First Strawberries by Joseph Bruchac

Preparation: None

Lesson:
1. Read The First Strawberries to your child.
2. Come up with Indian names for your child and for yourself using some of your attributes as would the Indians.

Pre-Math – Ten Little Indians

Materials: None

Preparation: None

Lesson:
1. Sing "Ten Little Indians" song with your child. Have them put up the proper amount of fingers as you sing the words.

Ten Little Indians
One little, two little, three little Indians
Four little, five little, six little Indians
Seven little, eight little, nine little Indians
Ten little Indian boys.

Ten little, nine little, eight little Indians
Seven little, six little, five little Indians
Four little, three little, two little Indians
One little Indian boy.

History – Native American Headbands

Materials: Construction paper
                 Crayons
                 Tape

Preparation:
1. Cut out feather shapes from several different colors of construction paper.
2. Cut out a strip of paper to use for the headband.

[handwritten: Cut into paper to make it look like feather]

Lesson:
1. Wrap the construction paper strip round your child's head to measure it.
2. Before taping it into a circle, let your child decorate their headband and their feathers with crayons.
3. Help your child tape their feathers to their headband.
4. Tape the headband into a circular shape.

Art – Rubber Glove Turkey

Materials: Clear rubber glove
                 Brown tissue paper
                 Red tissue paper
                 Popcorn
                 String or yarn

Preparation: None

Lesson:
1. Let your child stuff the four fingers with brown tissue paper.
2. Have them stuff the thumb with red tissue paper.
3. Let them fill the palm of the glove with popcorn.
4. Tie off the bottom for a cute turkey.

Gross Motor Skills – Skating on Ice

Materials: Wax paper
                 Rubber bands

Preparation: None

Lesson:
1. Wrap long pieces of wax paper up and around your child's shoes.
2. Anchor the pieces on their legs with rubber bands.
3. Let your child "ice skate" on the carpet.
4. Warn your child that they need to skate and not run because the "ice" is slippery.

Literature -
<u>A plump and perky turkey</u> by Teresa Bateman
<u>Run, Turkey run</u> by Diane Mayr
<u>Thanksgiving in the White House</u> by Gary Hines
<u>Turk and Runt</u> by Lisa Wheeler

Week Ten

Your theme for this week will be *Jack-o-Lanterns and Harvest Time.* You will be focusing on the following topics with your child:

English – The letter J
Pre-Math – Diamond and the number 5
Art – The color orange

Lesson Forty-Six – Monday

English: Recognition of the Letter J

Materials: Card stock
              Pumpkin seeds

Preparation: Cut a capital letter J out of card stock.

Lesson: Let your child glue pumpkin seeds all over their capital J.

Pre-Math – Seed Counting

Materials: Pumpkin seeds

Preparation: None

Lesson:
1. Put a handful of pumpkin seeds in front of your child.
2. Have them count out different amounts of seeds. Be sure to emphasize the number 5 since that is what you are focusing on this week.

Art – Indian Corn

Materials: Indian corn (several pieces)
              Different colors of paint (including orange)
              Paper plates
              Paper
              Paint smock or old shirt
              Newspapers

Preparation: Cover the work surface with newspapers. Put the different colors of paint on different paper plates.

Lesson:
1. Have your child put on their paint smock or an old shirt. Have them roll up their sleeves to minimize the mess.
2. Let your child dip their Indian corn into the paint and then roll it around on their paper.
3. This activity can be messy, so provide a lot of supervision. Your child will be able to make a very neat design.

Gross Motor Skills – The Pumpkin Grand Prize Game

Materials: Orange ping pong balls
              5 buckets or large bowls

Preparation: None

Lesson:
1. Line up the buckets in a vertical row.
2. Have your child stand at the end of the row and attempt to toss the ping pong balls into the buckets in succession.

Science – Easy Pumpkin Pudding

Materials: Vanilla pudding
              1 can of Libby's Easy Pumpkin Pie Mix
              A bowl
              A spoon

Preparation: None

Lesson:
1. Help your child to measure and place 1 cup of vanilla pudding into their bowl.
2. Help them to measure out 2 tsp of pie mix and put it into their bowl.
3. Let your child stir the ingredients together and then eat their pudding.

Literature -
<u>The Berenstain Bears and the prize pumpkin</u> by Stan & Jan Berenstain
<u>Biscuit visits the pumpkin patch</u> by Alyssa Satin Capucilli
<u>Franklin's pumpkin</u> by Sharon Jennings
<u>The garden that we grew</u> by Joan Holub

Lesson Forty-Seven – Tuesday

English – Peter Peter Pumpkin Eater

Materials: None

Preparation: None

Lesson:

1. Read Peter Peter Pumpkin Eater rhyme to your child:

> Peter Peter Pumpkin Eater,
> Had a wife and couldn't keep her.
> He put her in a pumpkin shell,
> And there he kept her very well.

2. Discuss the variety of homes we all live in. Peter lives in a pumpkin shell in this rhyme…

Pre-Math – Counting Corn

Materials: Egg container
Dried corn kernels
Marker

Preparation: Cut out individual egg sections and write the numbers 1 – 5 inside them.

Lesson:
1. Give your child a handful of corn.
2. Give them count the corn and put the correct amount in each section of the egg carton.
3. Be sure to give your child more corn than they need so that they will have to count the corn for each section.

Geography – State Map

Materials: State road map
                  Highlighter

Preparation: None

Lesson:
1. Give the road map of your state to your child.
2. Talk to them about where you live. Draw a star for them in that location.
3. Highlight two major cities in your state. Let your child trace with their finger all the different ways that they could get from one city to the next.
4. Let your child highlight the most direct route from where they live to the cities.
5. Depending on the ability of your child, you might want to then drive the route to one of these cities and help your child to navigate on the map.

Fine Motor Skills – Mr. Pumpkin Head

Materials: Small pumpkin
                  Mr. Potato Head pieces

Preparation: Poke some holes where the eyes, nose, mouth, hat and ears should be.

Lesson: Let your child decorate Mr. Pumpkin Head using the Mr. Potato Head pieces.

Science – Growing Pumpkin Vines

Materials: Small aquarium or glass bowl
                  Pumpkin seeds
                  Dirt
                  Black construction paper

Preparation: Cover one side of the aquarium with black paper.

Lesson:
1. Let your child plant pumpkin seeds around the perimeter of the aquarium or bowl.
2. Have your child water the seeds and measure the vines using yarn.
3. Compare the growth of the seeds on Day 1, Day 5, etc. until the vines have grown out the top of the aquarium.
4. Talk to your child about how the seeds on the side covered with black paper aren't growing as well as the other seeds. Let them try to figure out why (no sunlight, warmth, etc.)
5. Talk to your child about the roots, the leaves, the vines, and the flowers.

Literature -
<u>Harvest home</u> by Jane Yolen
<u>Harvest time</u> by Mercer Mayer
<u>My pumpkin</u> by Julia Noonan
<u>Oh my, pumpkin pie!</u> by Charles Ghigna

Lesson Forty-Eight – Wednesday

English – Flashcards

Materials: Flashcards for Letters A – J

Preparation: None

Lesson:
1. Let your child try to put the flashcards in alphabetical order.
2. Mix them up and have them try it again. Let them continue until they can do it quickly without struggling.

Pre-Math – Pumpkins in the Patch

Materials: Green construction paper
               Orange construction paper

Preparation:
1. Cut out 5 diamonds from the green paper and 5 pumpkins from the orange paper.
2. Write the numbers 1 – 5 on the diamonds.

Lesson:
1. Give your child the pumpkins.
2. Place one of the numbered diamonds on the table in front of your child. Ask them to plant the correct number of pumpkins in the pumpkin patch.
3. Continue playing this game until you have worked through each number.

Art – Pumpkin Patch Divine

Materials: Construction paper
                    Orange and green washable paint
                    Paint smocks or old shirts
                    Green marker

Preparation: None

Lesson:
1. Place the paper on a table in front of your child.
2. Have him or her make a fist with one hand.
3. Paint the top of the fist (fingers and knuckles) orange. Help your child press their fist onto the sheet of paper to resemble a pumpkin.
4. Repeat until the paper has as many pumpkins prints as desired.
5. Next, help your child to make a green fingerprint at the top of each pumpkin for a stem.
6. When the paint is dry, let your child use a green marker to add vines to the picture.

Fine Motor Skills – Pumpkin Puzzle

Materials: A pumpkin

Preparation:
1. Cut the top off and clean the seeds and pulp out of a pumpkin. Your child would probably love to help with this part.
2. Cut various shapes out of the pumpkin and reinsert them.

Lesson:
1. Take all of the pieces of out the pumpkin.
2. Let your child figure out where they go and reinsert them.

Science – Popcorn

Materials: Unpopped popcorn
                    Popcorn air popper

Preparation: None

Lesson:
1. Let your child feel the unpopped corn kernels.
2. Ask them to describe how they feel.
3. Pop some popcorn in the air popper.
4. Have your child feel the popped kernels and compare them to the unpopped ones.
5. Eat the popcorn.

Literature -
<u>Sixteen runaway pumpkins</u> by Dianne Ochiltree
<u>Tiny Tilda's pumpkin pie</u> by Susan Kantor
<u>Too many pumpkins</u> by Linda White
<u>Patty's pumpkin patch</u> by Teri Sloat

Lesson Forty-Nine – Thursday

English – A Maze-ing

Materials: Thanksgiving Maze

Preparation: Find a maze on the Internet and print off a copy – you can find great
              mazes at: holidays.kaboose.com/thanks-maze.html

Lesson: Have your child solve the maze. You can have them do several of these
              mazes if they enjoy doing them.

Pre-Math – Following Directions

Materials: Small wheeled vehicle (matchbox car, etc.)
              Green paint
              Orange paint
              Brown construction paper

Preparation: None

Lesson:
1. The goal of this lesson is to see how well your child can follow directions.
2. Ask your child to run their small wheeled vehicles through the paint and onto the
   construction paper (the dirt), creating "rows." These green rows become our
   vines.
3. Ask your child to dot pumpkins onto the vines using small brushes dipped in
   orange paint.

Music – Bible Action Songs

Materials: "Action Bible Songs" CD or DVD by the Cedarmont Kids or other CD of
              your choice

Preparation: None

Lesson: Listen to these songs with your child and help them to learn the motions
              and the words.

Fine Motor Skills – Pin the Stem on the Pumpkin

Materials: Orange construction paper
               Green construction paper
               Blindfold
               Tape

Preparation:
1. Cut out a large pumpkin from the orange construction paper.
2. Cut out stems from the green construction paper.
3. Hang the pumpkin up on the wall at about your child's shoulder height.

Lesson:
1. Tell your child they are going to try to put the stem as close to the right spot on the pumpkin as possible.
2. Hand your child a "pumpkin stem" with tape on the backside.
3. Blindfold your child.
4. Slowly spin them around 3 – 4 times.
5. Stop your child when they are facing the pumpkin and turn them loose to try to reach out and put the stem on the pumpkin.
6. Take their blindfold off and let them see how well they did.
7. Let them do this activity several times – they'll love it!

Science – Pumpkin Float

Materials: Pumpkin
               Paper
               Crayons

Preparation:
1. Make a graph with two columns and enough rows for you and all of your children to be able to take a guess.
2. Fill up the bathtub or another large container with water.

Lesson:
1. Talk to your child about how science is the act of learning by observing – tell them they are going to be doing a scientific experiment today.
2. Ask your child if they think a pumpkin would sink or float.
3. Record their response as well as your own on the graph.
4. Put the pumpkin in the water and see if it sinks or floats.

Literature -
<u>Pooh's pumpkin</u> by Isabel Gaines
<u>The pumpkin blanket</u> by Deborah Turney Zagwyn
<u>Pumpkin day, pumpkin night</u> by Anne Rockwell
<u>The pumpkin fair</u> by Eve Bunting

Lesson Fifty – Friday

Pre-Math – How Much Do They Weigh?

Materials: Small pumpkins and gourds
                Bathroom scale

Preparation: None

Lesson: Let your child weigh the pumpkins and gourds in different combinations
                to see which ones weigh the most, how much they weigh altogether, etc.

Art – Shaken Confetti

Materials: Several different colors of paper
                Glue
                Garbage bag or paper grocery bag
                Black marker

Preparation: Draw the shape of a pumpkin on one of the pieces of paper.

Lesson:
1. You and your child should rip up several colors of paper into small pieces and put it into the garbage bag.
2. Let your child cut the pumpkin out of their paper.
3. Have your child cover their pumpkin shape with glue.
4. Let your child put their pumpkin (with the wet glue) into the garbage bag and shake it all around. The confetti will stick to the pumpkin making a cute art project.

Fine Motor Skills – Pumpkin Pie Play-Doh

Materials: 5 1/2 cups flour
2 cups salt
8 teaspoon cream of tatar
3/4 cups oil
1 container (1 1/2 ounces) pumpkin pie spice
Orange food coloring (or 2 parts yellow, 1 part red)
4 cups water

Preparation:
1. Mix all of the ingredients together.
2. Cook and stir over medium heat until all of the lumps disappear.
3. Knead the dough on a floured surface until it is smooth.
4. Store in airtight container.

Lesson: Let your child play with the pumpkin Play-Doh.

Science – Inside of a Pumpkin

Materials: Pumpkin
Spoon
Bowl
Magnifying glass

Preparation: None

Lesson:
1. Cut the top off of a pumpkin.
2. Let your child explore the inside of the pumpkin using the spoon, bowl, magnifying glass and anything else they can dream up.

Literature -
Gourds by Kathleen Pohl.
Word Bird's Thanksgiving words by Jane Belk Moncure
Cornfield hide- and- seek by Christine Widman
Farmer Smart's fat cat by James Sage

Week Eleven

Your theme for this week will be *Kites and Wind*. You will be focusing on the following topics with your child:

English – The letter K
Pre-Math – Circles and the number 6
Art – The color red

Lesson Fifty-One – Monday

English: Recognition of the Letter K

Materials: Card stock
               Lipstick or colored lip balm

Preparation: Cut a capital letter K out of card stock.

Lesson: Have your child put on lipstick or colored lip balm and make kiss lip prints all over their letter K.

Pre-Math – Wallpaper Kits

Materials: Variety of wallpaper remnants

Preparation: Cut kite shapes out of wallpaper. Cut the kites in half.

Lesson: Give the kites to your child and let them try to match them up by their design.

Art and Gross Motor Skills – Paper Plate Kite

Materials: Paper plate
               Tissue paper
               Streamers
               Crayons
               String
               Craft sticks
               Long piece of yarn (maybe 5ft.)

Preparation: None

Lesson:
1. Have your child draw a design on their paper plate.
2. Let them use the tissue paper to enhance their design if they would like.
3. Have your child glue foot long streamers onto the tail end of the paper plate.
4. Punch a hole at the nose of the plate and tie some yarn through it.
5. Tape the other end of the yarn to a craft stick. Wrap the additional yarn between the stick and the kite around the craft stick as well.
6. Let your child take their kite outside on a windy day – it really should fly!
7. Save this kite for future lessons.

Science – What a Wind!

Materials: Ordinary items your child uses regularly (i.e., paper plate, sheet, leaves, etc.)

Preparation: None

Lesson:
1. Talk to your child about the wind. Ask them if they remember ever having had anything blow away from them.
2. On a really windy day, take your child outside and show them the effect that wind has on ordinary items they use regularly.

Literature -
Angel's kite by Alberto Blanco
The Berenstain bears and the big red kite by Stan & Jan Berenstain
Crosby by Dennis Haseley
Curious George flies a kite by Margaret Rey

Lesson Fifty-Two – Tuesday

English – Feel the Wind

Materials: A fan
                 Several ordinary items from around the house
                 Katie's too-big coat by Jane Stephens

Preparation: None

Lesson:
1. Talk to your child about the wind.
2. Turn on the fan at different levels so that they can feel the "wind" blowing at different speeds.
3. Read Katie's too-big coat to your child with the fan on.
4. Gather several items from around the house and place them in front of the fan to see if they blow in the wind.

Pre-Math – How Far did the Kite Fly

Materials: Paper plate kite (made in yesterday's lesson)
                 Tape measure
                 Stick (optional)

Preparation: None

Lesson:
1. Let your child fly their kite again.
2. When they're done, don't rewind the string to bring it down. Wrap the string around another stick or your hand.
3. When you get the kite down, stretch out the string to show your child how high up their kite was.
4. Measure how high up the kite was and then measure your child.
5. Tell your child how many children high their kite ended up. This will help them to put the height into perspective a bit better.

Geography – Color the Flag

Materials: A Blank Coloring Page of your country's map (check out
               www.abcteach.com/directory/researchreports/flags/country_flags/)
               A colored picture of the flag for your child to copy

Preparation: Find and print off a coloring page of your country's flag.

Lesson: Let your child color the flag using the correct colors.

Fine Motor Skills – Wind and Clouds

Materials: Straws
               Cotton balls

Preparation: None

Lesson: Have a cloud race with your child by blowing into a straw to move cotton
               balls across the table or floor.

Science - Kite Snack

Materials: Bread
               Butter
               Licorice string
               Plastic knife or cheese spreader

Preparation: None

Lesson:
   1. Help your child to cut the bread into the shape of a kite.
   2. Toast the bread.
   3. Let your child butter the bread.
   4. Add a licorice string as a tail.
   5. Let your child enjoy their snack.

Literature -
The flyaway kite by Steve Björkman
Hamlet and the enormous Chinese dragon kite by Brian Lies
The kite festival by Leyla Torres.
Riley flies a kite by Susan Blackaby

Lesson Fifty-Three – Wednesday

English – Trace the K

Materials: Handwriting Paper (for preschool age) – can print some out at this website: www.first-school.ws/theme/printables/writing-paper/handwriting.htm
Pencil
Yellow marker

Preparation: Using the yellow marker, write several capital K's and small k's on the handwriting paper.

Lesson:
1. Help your child to trace the K's with their finger. Be sure to explain to them how to properly form the letter.
2. Then ask your child to trace the K's with their pencil.
3. If your child's is able, have them practice forming some K's on their own.

Pre-Math – 6 Items – 3 Pairs

Materials: 6 mittens
6 socks
6 shoes
6 boots, etc.

Preparation: None

Lesson:
1. Talk to your child about what pairs are.
2. Then put a pile of everyday household items in front of them and see if they can determine which ones are pairs.

Gross Motor Skills – Windy Weather Catch

Materials: Blow dryer
Scarf, tissue, other light objects

Preparation: None

Lesson: Blow the light objects into the air one at a time and have your child try to catch them.

Science – Blow Soccer

Materials: Shoe box
              Marker
              Cotton ball

Preparation: Draw a line down the middle of the inside of the shoe box. Draw a goal
              area at each end.

Lesson: The Object of the game is to try to blow the cotton ball into your
              opponent's goal area while your opponent attempts to block you by
              blowing with his straw.

Literature -
The Sea-Breeze Hotel by Marcia Vaughan and Patricia Mullins
Someone bigger by Jonathan Emmett
Comes a wind by Linda Arms White
Elmer takes off by David McKee

Lesson Fifty-Four – Thursday

English: Go to the Library

Materials: None

Preparation: None

Lesson:
1. Go to the library.
2. Let your child pick out some books that he or she might enjoy.
3. Reading is so important! You should do everything you can to get your child excited about reading at a young age.

Pre-Math – Sandpaper Circles

Materials: Block of scrap wood
                Fine sandpaper (nothing too abrasive)

Preparation: Cut a large circle out of the sandpaper – one that is large enough for your child to use easily.

Lesson:
1. Give your child the wood and the sandpaper circle.
2. Ask them to sand the wood by moving their sandpaper in a circular motion.
3. Repeat a chant with your child while they work:

> "Round, round, and round we go;
> We can move fast or we can move slow."

Music – Red

Materials: None

Preparation: None

Lesson:
1. Sing this song with your child:

Red
(Tune: Someone's in the Kitchen with Dinah)

Red is the color of Apples.
Red is the color of Fire, too.
Red is the color of my heart.
I like red don't you?

Fine Motor Skills – Cutting Strips

Materials: Scissors
                Paper
                Ruler (optional)

Preparation: Draw vertical lines across the piece of paper.

Lesson:
1. Ask your child to cut on the lines, cutting the paper into strips.
2. You can increase the difficulty of this activity by giving your child a ruler and having them draw their own lines on their paper before they cut.

Science – Red Taste Test

Materials: Strawberries
                Raspberries
                Cherries
                Red apple
                Other red food
                Poster board
                Markers

Preparation: None

Lesson:
1. You and your child taste each of these foods.
2. Make a graph showing how many people liked each food.

Literature -
Hetty's new hat by Margaret Nash
How the ladies stopped the wind by Bruce McMillan
It's too windy! by Hans Wilhelm
Like a windy day by Frank Asch & Devin Asch

Lesson Fifty-Five – Friday

English – K, K, What Begins with K?

Materials: White board
                    Dry erase markers

Preparation: None

Lesson:
1. Discuss what sound the letter K makes.
2. Brainstorm with your child to come up with words that have that beginning sound and write them on the white board.
3. You can print letter K in a different bright color to make it stand out.

Pre-Math – Kite Counting

Materials: Construction paper
                    String

Preparation:
1. Cut a kite shape out of the construction paper.
2. Cut several bows out of the construction paper as well.
3. Tie the string to the bottom of your kite.

Lesson: Lay different numbers of bows on top of the kite string and help your child to count them.

Art – Kite Blots

Materials: Paper
                    Several colors of paint
                    Streamers

Preparation: Cut a large diamond out of the paper.

Lesson:
1. Help your child put dabs of paint on their kite.
2. Have your child fold their kite in half and then open it up. The paint will make a neat design.
3. Help them attach the streamer to be the kite's tail.

Fine Motor Skills – Lock and Unlock

Materials: Locks with keys (could be your door lock)

Preparation: None

Lesson: Let your child use the key to lock and unlock.

Science – Wind Stick

Materials: Empty paper towel roll
                        Several colors of tissue paper
                        Paint
                        Stapler

Preparation: None

Lesson:
1. Have your child paint the paper towel roll.
2. Have your child cut strips out of several colors of tissue paper.
3. Staple the tissue paper strips to the end of the roll.
4. On a particularly windy day, let your child take their project outside and watch the strips blow in the wind.

Literature -
One Monday by Amy Huntington
The village of the basketeers by Lynda Gene Rymond
What's the magic word? by Kelly DiPucchio
Whoosh went the wind! by Sally Derby

Week Twelve

Your theme for this week will be *laughing and other emotions*. You will be focusing on the following topics with your child:

English – The letter L
Pre-Math – Circles and the number 6
Art – The color purple

Lesson Fifty-Six – Monday

English: Recognition of the Letter L

Materials: Card stock
               Hole punch
               String

Preparation:
   1. Cut a capital letter L out of card stock.
   2. Punch holes around the entire outside edge of the L.

Lesson: Let your child use the string to lace the L.

Pre-Math – Classification Sorting

Materials: 6 paper clips
               6 buttons
               6 beads
               6 cotton balls
               6 dried beans
               6 pieces of macaroni
               A box
               Muffin tin

Preparation: Put all of the materials in the box.

Lesson: Let your child sort the objects by placing each kind of object into a separate muffin tin cup.

Art – Feelings Collage

Materials: Old magazines or newspaper inserts
                Scissors
                Construction paper
                Glue stick

Preparation: None

Lesson:
1. Have your child cut out people who are showing different emotions.
2. Have your child sort the people based on their emotions.
3. Let them make a collage with different areas of the paper representing the different emotions.

Gross Motor Skills – Ladder Coordination

Materials: A ladder

Preparation: None

Lesson:
1. Place the ladder flat on the ground.
2. Have your child do the following:
   a. Walk forward on the rungs
   b. Walk forward on the sides
   c. Walk forward in the spaces between the rungs

Literature -
Am I making God smile? by Jeannie St. John Taylor
The feel good book by Todd Parr
Happy to you! by Caron Lee Cohen
Hip, hip, hooray for Annie McRae! by Brad Wilcox

Lesson Fifty-Seven– Tuesday

English – Emotions Books

Materials: 3 Pieces of construction paper
                Stapler
                Black marker

Preparation:
1. Fold the paper in half to make a book and staple it together.
2. Write the following phrases on the pages:
   a. "My Emotions Book" on cover.
   b. "I feel happy when" on 1st page.
   c. "I feel sad when" on 2nd page.
   d. "I feel scared when" on 3rd page.
   e. "I feel angry when" on 4th page.
   f. "I feel surprised when" on 5th page.

Lesson:
1. Have your child dictate their answers to you and write them down for them.
2. Let them draw pictures to illustrate the pages – you may want to have them illustrate each page at a different time so that they will take time with their drawings.

Pre-Math – 6 Balls of Snow

Materials: White construction paper
                Blue construction paper
                Glue stick
                Crayons

Preparation: Cut out circles of various sizes from the white construction paper.

Lesson:
1. Instruct your child to create a snowman using 6 balls.
2. Have them try to count out the proper amount of balls themselves.
3. Let them glue their snowman to their paper.
4. Allow your child to color their pictures further.

Geography – Where I Live

Materials: Globe

Preparation: None

Lesson:
1. Help your child to identify their continent on the globe.
2. Help them to identify their country on the globe.
3. Help them to identify their state on the globe.
4. Help them to identify approximately where they live.
5. Point out any major features in or around your state (i.e., the Great Lakes for Michigan).

Fine Motor Skills – Drawing Lines

Materials: Paper
              Pencil

Preparation: None

Lesson: Have your child practice drawing horizontal lines across their paper.

Literature –
If you're happy and you know it! by Jan Ormerod & Lindsey Gardiner
Misery Moo by Jeanne Willis and Tony Ross
Polly Molly Woof Woof : a book about being happy by David Lloyd
Sun Jack & Rain Jack by Ursel Scheffler

Lesson Fifty-Eight– Wednesday

English – String of Friends

Materials: Paper
              Crayons

Preparation: Cut out a string of 6 paper dolls (without faces or details).

Lesson:
1. Give your child the string of paper dolls.
2. Let your child draw faces and whatever other details they would like.
3. Have them tell you who the people are (suggest they make them look like people in their family, friends, etc.)

Pre-Math – Match the Emotions

Materials: Paper
              Scissors
              Markers

Preparation:
1. Cut 20 circles out of the paper.
2. Make 2 copies of 10 faces with different emotions:
   a. Happy
   b. Sad
   c. Worried
   d. Scared (huge mouth in a horse shoe shape)
   e. Loving (kissing face)
   f. Stressed (big eyes and wiggly line for a mouth)
   g. Mad
   h. Silly
   i. Tired (drooping eyelids with yawning mouth)
   j. Surprised (big eyes with wide open mouth)

Lesson: Put the faces in front of your child and let them match them up into pairs.

Art – L Collage

Materials: Straws
              Construction paper
              Glue

Preparation: Cut long and short pieces of straw.

Lesson: Using the straws, let your child create an L collage on the construction paper.

Gross Motor Skills – Leapfrog

Materials: None

Preparation: None

Lesson: Play leapfrog with your child. Be sure to tuck yourself into the smallest shape possible to make it easier for your child to leapfrog over you.

Science – Comfort Cookies

Materials: 3 cups margarine
               3 cups brown sugar
               3 cups flour
               6 cups oats
               1 tablespoon baking soda
               2 cups chocolate drops (or butterscotch or peanut butter drops)

Preparation: None

Lesson:
1. Mash, knead, squeeze, pound, pinch, etc. all ingredients in a large bowl until completely blended.
2. Form into small balls about 1 to 1 1/2 inches in size and place on an ungreased cookie sheet.
3. Butter the bottom of a small juice glass and then dip it into white sugar, then pound the cookies flat with it.
4. Bake the cookies at 350 degrees for approx. 10-12 mins.

Literature -
Elmo's New Laugh by Christine Ferraro
Eight Silly Monkeys by Steve Haskamp
Mr. Gumpy's Outing by John Burningham
Today I Feel Silly by Jamie Lee Curtis

Lesson Fifty-Nine– Thursday

English – Expressions Album

Materials: Old magazines or newspaper inserts
                Construction paper
                Glue stick
                Stapler
                Marker

Preparation: Fold the construction paper into a book.

Lesson:
1. Help your child look for pictures of people showing emotions in the old magazines.
2. Let your child cut these people out.
3. Ask your child how they think each person is feeling.
4. Let your child glue the pictures into their Expressions Album.
5. Write the name of the emotion the person is expressing under each picture.

Pre-Math – Roll the Die

Materials: 1 Die

Preparations: None

Lesson:
1. Roll the die.
2. Have your child tell you what number comes up.
3. Have your child jump that many times, do that many somersaults, etc.

Music – "I've Got the Joy"

Materials: None

Preparation: None

Lesson: Sing this song with your child:

I've Got the Joy
I've got the joy, joy, joy, joy down in my heart.
Where? Down in my heart!
Where? Down in my heart!
I've got the joy, joy, joy, joy down in my heart,
Down in my heart to stay.

Chorus:
And I'm so happy. So very happy !
I've got the love of Jesus in my heart.
And I'm so happy so very happy
I've got the love of Jesus in my heart!

I've got the peace that passes understanding,
Down in my heart,
Where? Down in my heart!
Where? Down in my heart!
I've got the peace that passes understanding,
Down in my heart to stay.

I've got the love of Jesus, love of Jesus
Down in my heart,
Where? Down in my heart!
Where? Down in my heart!
I've the got love of Jesus, love of Jesus
Down in my heart to stay.

I've got the wonderful love of my precious redeemer way down in the depths of my heart,
Where? Down in the depths of my heart,
Where? Down in the depths of my heart.
I've got the wonderful love of my precious redeemer way down in the depths of my heart;
Down in the depths of my heart to stay!

Fine Motor Skills – Pickup Sticks

Materials: Set of pickup sticks

Preparation: None

Lesson: Play pickup sticks with your child.

Literature -
I Love My Mama by Peter Kavanagh
Sam Loves Kisses by Yves Got
Ella and the Naughty Lion by Anne Cottringer
The Very Lonely Firefly by Eric Carle

Lesson Sixty– Friday

English: Further Recognition of the Letter L

Materials: Paper
                    Lemon
                    Lime
                    Newspaper
                    Paint smock or old shirt

Preparation:
1. Cut a capital letter L out of paper.
2. Cut the lemon and lime into slices.

Lesson: Let your child "paint" their L with the lemon and lime slices.

Pre-Math – Snowflakes

Materials: White paper
                    Scissors

Preparation: Create some paper snowflakes – some with 6 points, some with more or
                    less points.

Lesson:
1. Let your child sort out the snowflakes by how many points they have.
2. Mark a large dot on one point of each snowflake so they'll know which point they
   started counting with.

Art – Easy Easel Project

Materials: Art easel w/ paper or 2 large pieces of paper taped to wall
                    Crayons

Preparation: None

Lesson: Ask your child to draw a happy face on one paper and a sad face on the
                    other paper.

Gross Motor Skills – Leg Rocks

Materials: None

Preparation: None

Lesson:
1. This lesson incorporates leg exercises for your child. Have him or her stand with their feet shoulder distance apart.
2. Ask your child to point their right toes forward lifting their foot off the floor.
3. As them to squeeze their leg muscles as hard as they can.
4. Have them make the calf muscle feel like a rock.
5. Have them touch it and see if they can make it even harder.
6. Then tell them to let it go mushy.
7. Have them do steps 2-6 with their left leg.
8. Have your child jump with both feet.
9. Ask if they can jump higher if they point their toes toward the floor.
10. Have them shake their legs one at a time so that they're loose like noodles.

Literature -
Taking a bath with the dog and other things that make me happy by Scott Menchin
What makes you happy? by Charnan Simon
The wonderful gift by Clare Bevan
Let's fly a kite by Stuart J. Murphy

Week Thirteen

Your theme for this week will be *All About ME*. You will be focusing on the following topics with your child:

English – The letter M
Pre-Math – Squares and the number 7
Art – The color yellow

Lesson Sixty-One– Monday

English: Recognition of the Letter M

Materials:	Card stock
	Colored macaroni
	Glue

Preparation: Cut a capital letter M out of card stock.

Lesson: Let your child glue macaroni all over their capital M.

Pre-Math – 7th Heart

Materials:	Red construction paper
	Heart stickers
	Crayons

Preparation: Draw a heart shape on the construction paper.

Lesson:
1. Have your child cut out the heart.
2. Allow them to put 7 stickers on their heart.
3. Let them color their heart.

Art – My Face

Materials: Hand-held mirror (look at thrift stores, flea markets, or garage sales)
               Paint

Preparation: None

Lesson:
   1. Have your child take a long look in the mirror.
   2. Let your child try to paint their own face on their mirror.

Gross Motor Skills – The Big Face

Materials: A large box
               Bean bags

Preparation:
   1. Draw a huge face on the box.
   2. Cut out the mouth, nose and eyes (be sure to make them fairly large openings.)

Lesson: Let your child attempt to throw the bean bags through the holes in the
               face.

Science – How Hearts Work

Materials: Red food coloring
               A clear balloon
               A straw
               A large bowl or bucket

Preparation: None

Lesson:
   1. Color some water red with the food coloring.
   2. Fill the balloon with the red water.
   3. Put a straw in the balloon.
   4. Show your child how our hearts pump by squeezing the balloon. Water will
      pump out similar to the way that our hearts pump blood through our bodies.

Literature –
Me on the Map by Joan Sweeney
You Can Do It, Sam by Amy Hest
All By Myself by Ivan Bates
A Child's Book of Manners by Ruth Shannon Odor

Lesson Sixty-Two– Tuesday

English – Snow White and the Seven Dwarfs

Materials: Any version of the <u>Snow White and the Seven Dwarfs</u> book

Preparation: None

Lesson:
1. Read the book to your child, stopping often to count the dwarfs.
2. You can also act out the story afterwards with your child.

Pre-Math – Counting/Patterning

Materials: Pink construction paper
               Gray construction paper
               White construction paper

Preparation: Cut out 7 pink hearts and 7 gray hearts.

Lesson:
1. Have your child glue the hearts to the paper in a pattern – pink, gray, pink, gray, etc.
2. Ask your child to repeat the pattern with you.
3. Have them tell you which color heart would come next.
4. You can increase the difficulty of this lesson by including red hearts as well (pink, gray, red, pink, gray, red, etc.)

Fine Motor Skills – Smiley Face Necklaces

Materials: Construction paper
               Crayons/markers
               Hole punch
               Noodles
               Yarn
               Glue

Preparation: Cut out a circle shape from the construction paper.

Lesson:
1. Have your child draw a face on paper.
2. Punch two holes near the top of the circle.
3. Give your child the noodles, yarn and the crayons to decorate their smiley face.
4. Once the glue dries, let your child thread their smiley face onto the yarn and help them tie it around their neck to make a necklace.

Science – The Parts of our Face

Materials: A printout of a face (there is a good one at the following website:
                    www.enchantedlearning.com/subjects/anatomy/body/labelface/)
                    Crayons

Preparation: None

Lesson:
1. Help your child to label the different parts of the face.
2. Let your child color their face picture.
3. Review the parts of the face through the day – as well as the rest of the week.

Literature –
The Foot Book by Dr. Seuss
The Nose Book by Al Perkins
The Tooth Book by Theo. LeSieg
Me and My Family Tree by Joan Sweeney

Lesson Sixty-Three– Wednesday

English – My Profile

Materials: Long paper
                      Markers or crayons
                      Colored construction paper (optional)
                      Yarn (optional)

Preparation: None

Lesson:
1. Lay out a piece of paper on the floor which is a little bit longer than your child is tall.
2. Have your child lay down sideways on the paper with their hands at their sides.
3. Use a marker to trace around your child – you will record their profile since they are lying on their side.
4. Use the materials to help your child to decorate their profile.
5. Hang their profile up on the wall for them to enjoy.

Pre-Math – Square Squat Game

Materials: Newspaper or other cheap paper
                      "Play A Little: 15 Action Songs For Little Ones" or other music of your choice

Preparation:
1. Cut large shapes from the paper – include several squares.
2. Tape the shapes to the floor
3. Turn on the music. Have your child move from one shape to the other.
4. Each time the music stops, tell them to quickly move to a square and squat.

Science – Body Parts Dice

Materials: A medium to large box
                      Old magazines or newspaper inserts
                      Glue

Preparation: Paste pictures of body parts to the different sides of the box.

Lesson:
1. Let your child roll the dice.
2. Have them point to whatever body part is rolled and say its name.

Gross Motor Skills – My Heartbeat

Materials: Stethoscope (or make your own with toilet paper rolls)

Preparation: None

Lesson:
1. Let your child listen to your heartbeat.
2. Listen to your child's heartbeat.
3. Exercise for a few minutes and then listen to the heartbeats again to hear how much faster they are.

Snack – Gingerbread People

Materials: Gingerbread man cookies

Lesson: Let your child identify the different body parts on the gingerbread man before they eat him.

Literature -
From Head to Toe by Eric Carle
I'm Glad to be Me by P.K. Hallinan
Just Me by Marie Hall Ets
Billy The Littlest One by Miriam Schlein

Lesson Sixty-Four– Thursday

English – All About Me Book

Materials: Construction paper
                     Washable ink pad
                     Old magazines or newspaper inserts
                     Glue stick
                     Measuring tape
                     Bathroom scale

Preparation: Using 3 pieces of construction paper, fold them and staple them to make a book. Write these words on the pages:
1. "All About Me Book" (on the title page)
2. "A Self-Portrait" (on page 1)
3. "My Fingerprints are Unique" (on page 2)
4. "My Favorite Color" (on page 3)
5. "I Am Special" (on page 4)
6. "Name: _____
   Age: _____
   Height: _____
   Weight: _____" (on page 5)

Lesson:
1. Your child is going to make a book that is all about them at this particular point in time. You need to help them to
   a. Page 1 – Have them draw a self-portrait
   b. Page 2 – Have them put their fingerprints around the page in the shape of a square
   c. Page 3 – Let your child cut out pictures from the old magazine which are in their favorite color – making a collage
   d. Page 4 – Trace your child's hand on the page
   e. Page 5 – Let your child write their name if they are able, and help them to record the rest of the information on their page.

Music – Old Favorites

Materials: Music CD (optional)

Preparation: None

Lesson:
1. Do the Hokey Pokey with your child.
2. Sing "Oh Be Careful Little Eyes" with your child.

Gross Motor Skills – My Body Parts

Materials: None

Preparation: None

Lesson: Ask your child to locate the different parts of their body (head, back, elbow, nose, wrist, feet, ankles, shoulders, stomach, etc.)

Art – The Me Puppet

Materials: Paper lunch bags
               Crayons
               Fabric scraps
               Yarn

Preparation: None

Lesson:
1. Let your child make a puppet that resembles them.
2. Your child can create their facial features on the bag and use the yarn for hair.
3. Let them use the fabric scraps to make "clothes" for their puppet.

Literature -
If the Shoe Fits by Alison Jackson
Just Me and My Dad by Mercer Mayer
A. Lincoln and Me by Louise Borden & Ted Lewin
Farm Flu by Teresa Bateman

Lesson Sixty-Five– Friday

English – Writing My Name

Materials: Handwriting paper
                 Pencil

Preparation: None

Lesson: Let your child practice writing their name on their paper. If your child struggles with this skill, write their name for them with yellow marker and let your child trace it instead.

Pre-Math – Counting Me

Materials: Paper
                 Crayons

Preparation: Create a graph with columns for different body parts (i.e., head, hands, fingers, toes, arms, etc.)

Lesson:
1. Have your child count out the different body parts that are on their graph.
2. Help them to color the appropriate number of squares for each body part.

Art – My ME Quilt

Materials: Construction paper
                 Crayons or markers
                 Glue stick
                 Cardboard
                 Large picture of your child

Preparation:
1. Cut the construction paper into squares.
2. Cut your child's picture into the same sized squares.

Lesson: Have your child make a quilt by gluing squares of construction paper and squares of their picture onto the cardboard.

Fine Motor Skills – My Thumbprint

Materials: Pictures of fingerprints (search for these on the internet)
               2 cups flour
               1 teaspoon salt
               1/2 cup margarine
               1/4 cup water
               Fruit preserves or jelly

Preparation: None

Lesson:
1. Show your child the pictures of fingerprints. Discuss with them the fact that all people have unique fingerprints.
2. Help your child mix together the flour, salt margarine and water until a stiff dough is formed.
3. Give your child a piece of the dough to roll into a ball.
4. Then have your child press their thumbs into it to make a "print".
5. Place these on a cookie sheet and bake at 350 degrees for 8-10 minutes.
6. When they come out of the oven, let your child spoon some fruit preserves into their fingerprint before eating it.

Science – Your Spine

Materials: An empty egg carton
               A few Kleenexes

Preparation: Cut apart the sections of the egg carton and stack them putting tissue between each piece of "cartilage".

Lesson:
1. Explain to your child how our spine works and then show them with the "spine" that you've created.
2. The stack of egg cartons should move similarly to the way our spines move.
3. Let your child feel your spine – and their own spine.

Literature -
The Big Sneeze by Ruth Brown
God Gave Us You by Lisa Tawn Bergren
Not so Rotten Ralph by Jack Gantos
Is Your Mama a Llama? by Deborah Guarino

Your theme for this week will be *nursery rhymes*. You will be focusing on the following topics with your child:

English – The letter N
Pre-Math – Squares and the number 7
Art – The color green

Lesson Sixty-Six– Monday

English: Recognition of the Letter N

Materials: Card stock
                 Dried noodles
                 Glue

Preparation: Cut a capital letter N out of card stock.

Lesson: Let your child glue the dried noodles all over their capital N.

Pre-Math – Magic Frog

Materials: Frog outline (see companion download)
                 Yellow construction paper
                 Blue bingo marker or regular blue marker

Preparation: Print the frog from the companion download onto yellow
                 construction paper. Cut it out.

Lesson:
   1. Let your child put dots on their frog with the blue bingo marker.
   2. It will be "magical" to them to see the dots turn green.
   3. (Optional) If your child is able, you can let them cut their own frog out at this
      point.

Art – Egg Painting

Materials: A Child's Treasury of Nursery Rhymes by Kady MacDonald Denton
              Paper
              A few eggs
              Food coloring (optional)

Preparation: None

Lesson:
   1. Read Humpty Dumpty to your child from the book.
   2. Let your child paint with the egg white. You might want to add food coloring to the "paint."

Gross Motor Skills – Nursery Rhyme Skit

Materials: None

Preparation: None

Lesson: Have your child act out all of their favorite nursery rhymes.

Science – Magnetic Humpty Dumpty

Materials: Plastic Easter eggs
              Metal screws, washers, etc.
              Paint
              A few magnets
              Blocks

Preparation: Put the screws and washers inside the plastic eggs.

Lesson:
   1. Let your child paint a few of the eggs.
   2. Let your child build a wall with the blocks.
   3. After the paint dries, let your child experiment with them while reciting the Humpty Dumpty nursery rhyme. Have them put an egg on a block (a wall) and use the magnet to get Humpty to lean over, fall backwards, tip sideways, or "have a great fall."

Literature –
A Child's Treasury of Nursery Rhymes by Kady MacDonald Denton
Gingerbread Baby by Jan Brett
The Little Red Hen by Jean Horton Berg
The Complete Tales of Peter Rabbit and other Favorite Stories by Beatrix Potter

Lesson Sixty-Seven– Tuesday

English: Blind Pick

Materials: Poster board or large piece of construction paper
Thick blue marker

Preparation: Write several different numbers (0-7), letters (A-N), and all shapes studied on the poster board with the marker.

Lesson:
1. Have your child cover their eyes and point at the poster board.
2. See if your child can identify whatever number, letter or shape at which they are pointing.
3. Do this several times until they have identified several of the different objects.
4. If they haven't pointed to all of the numbers and letters that you've covered, individually point these out and have them identify each of them.

Pre-Math – Spider Legs

Materials: Black poster board
Colored clothespins

Preparation: Cut out a large spider from the poster board.

Lesson:
1. Tell your child how many legs the spider should have and let them attach the correct number of clothespins to the spider.
2. Do this several times in random order with varying numbers of legs.
3. Have your child count out loud as they attach the clothespins.

Art – Green Finger Paint

Materials: Ziploc bag
                     White shaving cream
                     Green food coloring

Preparation: None

Lesson:
1. Let your child squirt the shaving cream inside the bag.
2. Add a few drops of food coloring and close the bag making sure all of the air is out.
3. Give the bag to your child and let them squish it to mix all of the ingredients together.
4. (optional) You can cut a corner of the bag and let your child finger paint with the mixture if you would like.

Music – Counting Finger Play

Materials: None

Preparation: None

Lesson: Do the Rhyme "One, Two, Buckle My Shoe" with your child – having them put up the correct number of fingers.

One two buckle my shoe.
Three, four, shut the door.
Five, six, pickup sticks.
Seven, eight, lay them straight.
Nine, ten, a big fat hen.

Fine Motor Skills – Curds and Whey

Materials: Disposable paper bowl
                     White paper
                     Scissors
                     Glue

Preparation: Cut the paper into strips.

Lesson:
1. Have your child cut snips from the strips of paper.
2. Let them glue the snips all over the inside of their bowl to resemble curds and whey.

Science – Little Miss Muffet

Materials: Black licorice
              Chocolate cupcakes
              Mini marshmallows

Preparation: None

Lesson:
1. Have your child poke the black licorice into the cupcake to be the spider legs.
2. Let them use mini marshmallows to be the spider eyes.
3. Let your child enjoy their snack.

Literature -
The Gingerbread Man by Karen Schmidt
The Little Dog Laughed and Other Nursery Rhymes by Lucy Cousins
The Lucy Cousins Book of Nursery Rhymes by Lucy Cousins
The Three Bears by Byron Barton

Lesson Sixty-Eight– Wednesday

English – Nosey Picture

Materials: Old magazines or newspaper inserts
              Scissors
              Construction paper
              Glue stick

Preparation: None

Lesson:
1. Have your child find pictures of noses from the magazines.
2. Let them glue their noses to the construction paper to make a collage of noses.

Pre-Math – Fabric Sort

Materials: Fabric scraps

Preparation: None

Lesson: Give your child a pile of fabric scraps and let them sort them by pattern
              (stripes, polka-dots, plaids, etc.)

Art – Three Pigs House

Materials: Red paper
              Twigs
              Spaghetti or straw
              Glue
              Paint
              Construction paper
              Glue

Preparation: Cut small rectangles out of the red paper. Draw three large house shapes
              on the construction paper.

Lesson: Let your child create the houses of the Three Pigs by using the red paper
              rectangles for bricks, the spaghetti or straw for straw, and the small twigs
              for sticks.

Gross Motor Skills – Nursery Rhyme Role Play

Materials: Props for Nursery Rhymes

Preparation: None

Lesson: Let your child act out their favorite nursery rhymes. Here are some examples:
  i. Jack Be Nimble – let your child jump over an ordinary classroom item
  ii. Little Miss Muffet – let your child pretend to eat when a spider comes along and they get frightened away
  iii. Little Bo Peep – hide a toy sheep around the room and let your child search for it

Science – Playing with Pairs

Materials: Several pairs of gloves and mittens in various sizes and colors

Preparation: None

Lesson:
  1. Talk to your child about right versus left.
  2. Let your child practice putting them on and taking them off.
  3. Let your child sort them all by color.
  4. Let them sort them by size.
  5. Sort them by whether they are gloves or mittens.

Literature -
The three little pigs retold and illustrated by David McPhail
The top secret files of Mother Goose! by Gabby Gosling
Mother Goose rhyme time : people by Kimberly K. Faurot
20 hungry piggies by Trudy Harris

Lesson Sixty-Nine– Thursday

English – Horns to Blow

Materials: Empty toilet paper roll
              Wax paper
              Rubber band

Preparation: None

Lesson:
1. Let your child make a kazoo by covering the end of the toilet paper roll with wax paper and securing it with a rubber band.
2. Let them blow on their kazoo.

Pre-Math – Boy Blue and Haystack

Materials: Paper
              Crayons or markers
              Scissors

Preparation: Draw a haystack on the paper. Draw a boy on the paper and cut him out.

Lesson: Review spatial concepts with your child by putting Little Boy Blue "on the haystack," "under the haystack," "beside the haystack," etc.

Music – If You're Happy…

Materials: Kazoo made earlier in the day

Preparation: None

Lesson: Sing the song with your child. Let them play their kazoo off and on as well.

If You're Happy and You Know It
If you're happy and you know it, clap your hands (clap clap)
If you're happy and you know it, clap your hands (clap clap)
If you're happy and you know it, then your face will surely show it
If you're happy and you know it, clap your hands. (clap clap)

Verse two - …stomp your feet
Verse three - … shout amen
Verse four - … do all three

Fine Motor Skills – Decorate a Star

Materials: Cardboard
                   Aluminum foil
                   Tissue paper
                   Glue

Preparation: Cut a star shape out of the cardboard.

Lesson:
1. Let your child wrap their star with the aluminum foil.
2. Give your child the tissue paper. Let them rip it up and wad it and glue it onto their star.

Science – Haystacks

Materials: Styrofoam cup
                   Hay or yellow yarn
                   Glue

Preparation: Cut down the open end of the cup to make it shorter.

Lesson: Have your child glue the yarn or the hay all over the outside of their cup so that it will resemble a haystack.

Literature -
Clap your hands : finger rhymes by Sarah Hayes
The house that Jack built by Jeanette Winter
Knick-knack paddywhack by Emily Bolam
Mary had a little lamb by Sarah Josepha Hale

Lesson Seventy– Friday

English – Calendar

Materials: This month's calendar page (you can print this from Microsoft Word)

Preparation: None

Lesson:
1. Talk to your child about different concepts of time.
    a. Tell them what month and date it is.
    b. Talk to them about the days of the week.
    c. Talk to them about morning, noon and evening.
    d. Talk to them about day and night.
    e. Talk to them about then and now.
    f. Talk to them about yesterday, today, and tomorrow.
2. Have your child color different squares on the calendar which correspond to different days of the week (i.e., color all of the Mondays blue, etc.)

Pre-Math – Watchmaker Game

Materials: None

Preparation: None

Lesson:
1. Stand on the opposite side of the room as your child.
2. You are the watchmaker. When the watchmaker says "2 o'clock," have your child take 2 steps. When the watchmaker says "10 o'clock," have your child take that many steps.
3. When the watchmaker says "12 o'clock," your child should start running and you can try to catch him or her.

Art – Jack's Candle

Materials: <u>A Child's Treasury of Nursery Rhymes</u> by Kady MacDonald Denton
Empty paper towel roll
Red tissue paper
Crayons or markers
Tape or glue

Preparation: None

Lesson:
1. Have your child decorate their tube to look like a candle using the crayons or other craft items you desire.
2. Let your child add the red tissue paper to be the flame.

Gross Motor Skills – Jack Jumping

Materials: Candle made earlier

Preparation: None

Lesson:
1. Recite the rhyme several times.
2. Let your child act out the rhyme by jumping over their candlestick.

Jack Be Nimble,
Jack Be Quick.
Jack Jumped Over the Candlestick.

Science – What Happened to Jack's Candle?

Materials: 2 Small candles (i.e., birthday candles)
                    Clear jar
                    Play-Doh
                    Squirt bottle filled with water

Preparation: None

Lesson:
1. Show your child the parts of the candle (wick and wax.)
2. Talk to them about the 3 things that fire needs to burn – heat, oxygen, and fuel.
3. Stand the candle up in the Play-Doh. Light the candle. Put the clear jar over the candle and watch how once all of the air is burned out from underneath the jar the candle will go out.
4. Ask your child what went away to cause the candle to burn out. (oxygen)
5. Stand the candle up in the Play-Doh again. You may want to cut the candle so that it is very small. Light the candle and watch how once all of the wax is gone the candle will go out.
6. Ask your child what went away to cause the candle to burn out this time. (fuel)
7. Stand the 2nd candle up in the Play-Doh. Light the candle. Squirt the candle with water and watch how the candle will again go out.
8. Ask your child what went away to cause the candle to burn out this time. (heat)

Literature -
The real Mother Goose book of American rhymes by Debby Slier
A play's the thing by Aliki
Three little kittens by Tanya Linch
The web files by Margie Palatini

Week Fifteen

Your theme for this week will be *oceans and whales*. You will be focusing on the following topics with your child:

English – The letter O
Pre-Math – Triangles and the number 8
Art – The color blue

Lesson Seventy-One – Monday

English: Recognition of the Letter O

Materials: Card stock
Oatmeal
Glue

Preparation: Cut a capital letter O out of card stock.

Lesson: Let your child glue the oatmeal all over their capital O.

Pre-Math – How Long is a Whale?

Materials: 100 ft. rope or a long tape measure

Preparation: None

Lesson:
1. Tell your child that a blue whale is about 100 feet long.
2. Let your child unwind the rope. They will be amazed at how long a blue whale is.
3. Ask your child to guess how many of their lengths it would take to make a blue whale.
4. Let your child lay down in the rope to measure them.
5. Then wind the rope back in to determine how many of them it would take to equal the length of the blue whale.

Art – Sand Picture

Materials: Sand
                  Glue
                  Construction paper
                  Newspaper

Preparation: None

Lesson:
1. Spread newspaper over the working area.
2. Help your child to draw a design or ocean scene on the construction paper.
3. Let your child apply glue along the outlines of the design.
4. Help your child to pour sand onto the glue and allow it to dry.
5. Help your child to gently shake their picture over a wastebasket to remove the excess sand.

Gross Motor Skills – Balloon Fish

Materials: Water balloons
                  Fishnets (optional)
                  Large bucket or bin

Preparation: Fill some balloons with water. Draw on fins, mouths, etc.

Lesson: Let your child play with these balloons inside the bucket. For added fun, let them use a fishnet to try to catch the fish.

Science – Float or Sink?

Materials: Normal household items
                  Large bucket or bin

Preparation: Fill the bucket with water. Gather the household items.

Lesson:
1. Hold up the items one at a time.
2. Ask your child if they think the item will float or sink.
3. Let your child toss it into the bin to see if it floats or sinks.

Literature -
Amanda explores the ocean by Maggie Smith
The best restaurant in the world by Michelle Schwarz
Bright Stanley by Matt Buckingham
Dear fish by Chris Gall

Lesson Seventy-Two – Tuesday

English – Ocean Concentration

Materials -   Ocean stickers (two sets – or one set if there are
                duplicates)
                Unlined index cards

Preparation:
1. Cut the index cards in half to make them more square.
2. Attach the stickers to the index cards. Be sure you have two cards with each type of sticker.

Lesson:
1. Lay the cards face down.
2. Take turns with your child turning up cards and trying to find a match.
3. Play this game just like the regular Concentration Game.

Pre-Math – Octopus Tentacle Match

Materials: Construction paper
                 Markers

Preparation:
1. Make a large octopus head out of the construction paper.
2. Write 8 different numbers or letters around the head.
3. Make 8 tentacles out of the construction paper and write the corresponding numbers or letters on the tentacles.

Lesson:
1. Have your child match the tentacles to the correct spot on the octopus head.

Art – Rainbow Fish

Materials: Coffee filter
                 Markers
                 Spray bottle filled with water
                 Newspapers

Preparation: Cut the coffee filter into the shape of a fish.

Lesson:
1. Cover the work surface with newspapers.
2. Have your child color their fish darkly with markers.
3. Let your child spray their fish with the water and watch the marker colors run.

Fine Motor Skills – Catch a Fish

Materials: Wooden spoon
Yarn
Magnet
Paperclips
Fish outline (see Companion Download)
Construction paper

Preparation:
1. Make a fishing pole out of the spoon, the yarn and the magnet.
2. Using the fish outline, print and cut out several fish.
3. Write letters or numbers or shapes on the bellies of the fish (whatever you'd like to work on with your child.)
4. Clip a paperclip onto the mouth area of each of the fish.

Lesson:
1. Spread out the fish on the floor in front of your child.
2. Let them try to catch a fish.
3. Have them identify what is written on each fish that they catch.
4. Let them throw it back and try to catch another fish.

Science – Diving Fish

Materials: Empty 2-liter bottle
Permanent marker
White vinegar
Baking soda
Raisins

Preparation: Using the marker, draw sea shapes on the outside of the 2-liter (seaweed, waves, fish, etc.).

Lesson:
1. Fill the bottle mostly full with water.
2. Add about ¼ cup of vinegar and 1 tsp of baking soda to the bottle.
3. Drop a small handful of raisin's into the bottle and watch what happens.
4. The chemical reaction from the vinegar and the baking soda will cause the raisins to collect bubbles around them, float to the top, sink back down, and collect more bubbles.

Literature –
The rainbow fish by Marcus Pfister
The dory story by Jerry Pallotta
Going on a journey to the sea by Jane Barclay
Hello, Ocean by Pam Muñoz Ryan

Lesson Seventy-Three – Wednesday

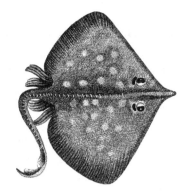

English – Draw the Ocean Waves

Materials: Paper
                Crayon or pencil

Preparation: None

Lesson: Have your child practice drawing wavy lines on the paper – like ocean waves.

Pre-Math – Whale Match Game

Materials: Pictures of whales (a good website for this is animals.nationalgeographic.com/animals/photos/whales/orca-killer-whale_image.html)
                Index cards

Preparation: Write down the names of the whales on the index cards.

Lesson:
1. Show your child each whale picture and show them the name of the whale as well.
2. Review the whales with them several times.
3. Then lay out the whale pictures on the floor and see if your child can identify each type of whale. They can either point to the name of the whale on the cards or give their answers orally.

Geography – Oceans

Materials: Map of the world (see companion download)
                Crayons

Preparation: Print the world map from the companion download.

Lesson:
1. Help your child to label the different oceans (Arctic, Atlantic, Indian, Pacific, and Southern)
2. Let your child color the oceans.

Gross Motor Skills – Feed the Shark

Materials: Cardboard or a large box
                  Paper
                  Beanbags
                  Marker

Preparation:
1. Draw a large shark on a piece of cardboard or the side of a box.
2. Cut a hole out where the shark's mouth would be. Make sure the hole is at least twice the size of a beanbag.
3. Add paper teeth.
4. Tape the board to a chair or set the box in the middle of the floor.

Lesson: Let your child try to feed the shark by throwing bean bags into its mouth.

Science – Magnified Shells and Sand

Materials: Several shells
                  Some sand
                  Magnifying glass

Preparation: None

Lesson: Let your child examine the shells and the sand with the magnifying glass.

Literature -
Can you hear the sea? by Judy Cumberbatch
Old shell, new shell : a coral reef tale by Helen Ward
Baby whale's journey by Jonathan London
Jean Laffite and the big ol' whale by Frank G. Fox

Lesson Seventy-Four – Thursday

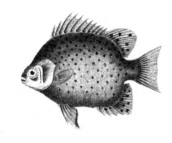

English – A School of Funny Fish

Materials: Photos of several family members
                    Various colors of construction paper
                    Glue stick

Preparation: Cut the faces out of the pictures.

Lesson:
1. Talk to your child about what it would be like to be a fish and live underwater. How would it feel to breathe through gills and not be able to talk? What kind of fish would they like to be? Where would they live and what would they eat?
2. Let your child draw and color a fish.
3. Let them glue their fish to a piece of blue construction paper.
4. Let your child glue the photo faces onto their fish.
5. Let your child dictate a short description about their life as a fish.

Pre-Math – Collecting By Likeness

Materials: Paper lunch bag
                    Various shapes and colors of blocks

Preparation: None

Lesson:
1. Give your child the paper bag and have him or her fill it with various blocks by likeness (i.e., "all of the triangle blocks", "all of the blue blocks", etc.)
2. As they put each item in the bag, have them explain to you why it belongs in the bag (what it has in common with the other items.)

Art – 3D Whale

Materials: Construction paper
Cotton balls
Glitter
Glue
Stapler or tape
Tissue paper
Googly eyes
Yarn
Paint

Preparation: Cut out two whale shapes from the construction paper.

Lesson:
1. Let your child decorate their whale however they'd like (i.e., outline the gills with glue and sprinkle glitter on them, etc.)
2. Let their project dry.
3. Help your child connect the two halves of their whale using the stapler or tape.
4. When only a small opening remains, let your child stuff cotton balls into their whale.
5. Then finish closing up the hole.

Fine Motor – Decorative Shells

Materials: Large pasta shells
Paint

Preparation: None

Lesson:
1. Explain to your child that no two shells are exactly alike.
2. Give your child the large pasta shells.
3. Let them paint the shells any way they would like.

Science – Salt Water Experiment

Materials: 2 glass jars
                Kosher salt
                2 hard-boiled eggs

Preparation: None

Lesson:
1. Fill one jar with water and one jar with water plus 4 Tbsp. of salt.
2. Put a hard-boiled egg in each jar.
3. Compare what happens to each egg.
4. Continue adding salt to the salt-water jar until the egg floats in the middle of the jar.

Literature -
Peg and the whale by Kenneth Oppel
The snail and the whale by Julia Donaldson
Willie the whale by Joy Oades
What the sea saw by Stephanie St. Pierre

Lesson Seventy-Five – Friday

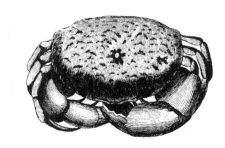

English – My Sea Creature Book

Materials: Construction paper
                    Crayons or markers
                    Stapler

Preparation: Fold the construction paper in half to make a book. Staple the binding.

Lesson:
1. Let your child dictate a story to you on the construction paper.
2. Have them illustrate their story.
3. Be sure to have them give their story a title.

Pre-Math – Ordering

Materials: Several different seashells

Preparation: None

Lesson:
1. Spread the seashells out in front of your child.
2. Have them put the shells in order:
   a. From smallest to largest
   b. From shortest to longest
   c. From thinnest to thickest
   d. From lightest to darkest, etc.

Geography – Ocean in a Bottle

Materials: Empty peanut butter jar
                    Pebbles
                    Plastic sea creatures
                    Salt
                    Super glue (optional)

Preparation: Remove the label from the jar.

Lesson:
1. Let your child put the small rocks in the jar.
2. Have them put the sea creatures in the jar.
3. Have them add water and sprinkle salt into the jar.
4. You will either want to supervise well or super glue the lids shut so that your child won't open it up.

Fine Motor Skills – Seashell Imprints

Materials: Play-Doh
                    Various shells and other ocean items (sea horse, starfish, etc.)

Preparation: None

Lesson: Give your child the Play-Doh and some shells. Let them experiment by making prints with their ocean items.

Science – Taste Salt Water

Materials: Salt
                    2 glasses of water

Preparation: Mix salt into one of the glasses of water.

Lesson:
1. Talk to your child about how the oceans have salt water in them and that we shouldn't drink that kind of water – it will make us more thirsty than not drinking at all.
2. Let your child take a small sip of the salt water.
3. Let your child take a sip of the regular water.
4. Have them describe to you what the salt water tasted like. Which one did they prefer?

Literature -
Way down deep in the deep blue sea by Jan Peck
Sneakers, the seaside cat by Margaret Wise Brown
Sam at the seaside by Mary Labatt
"Only joking!" laughed the lobster by Colin West

Week Sixteen

Your theme for this week will be *popcorn and pizza*. You will be focusing on the following topics with your child:

English – The letter P
Pre-Math – Circles and the number 8
Art – The color white

Lesson Seventy-Six – Monday

English: Recognition of the Letter P

Materials: Card stock
                  Popped popcorn
                  Glue

Preparation: Cut a capital letter P out of card stock.

Lesson: Let your child glue the popcorn all over their capital P.

Pre-Math – Mr. Eight

Materials: Construction paper
                  Glue stick
                  Various art supplies

Preparation: Cut a large 8 out of the construction paper.

Lesson:
1. Provide your child with a variety of art supplies.
2. Let your child glue their 8 onto some construction paper and then turn it into a person.
   a. The top circle can be his face.
   b. The arms and legs can be drawn or created from different art supplies.
3. Let your child create their own version of Mr. Eight. You might suggest to them that since he is made out of an 8 that he could have 8 of something (i.e., 8 eyes, 8 arms, etc.)

Art – School Pizza

Materials: Construction paper
                    Red paint
                    Yarn
                    Various art supplies

Preparation: Cut a large circle out of the construction paper.

Lesson:
1. Let your child make a pizza.
    a. They can paint red on it for pizza sauce
    b. Add yarn for cheese
    c. Add pink triangles for ham
    d. Add buttons for pepperoni
    e. There is no limit to the types of toppings your child can add.
2. After it dries, slice the pizza in half and talk to your child about halves and wholes.
3. Slice it further and talk about ¼ and 1/8. Your child probably won't fully understand these concepts, but it's great to start introducing them at this age anyway.

Gross Motor Skills – Topping Toss

Materials: Pizza pieces from above art lesson
                    Pizza pan
                    Masking tape (optional)

Preparation: None

Lesson:
1. Give your child their pizza slices and let them try to toss them into the pizza pan.
2. If your child has a hard time remembering to stand back far enough, you can make a starting line out of masking tape.

Science – White Snow

Materials: Snow
               Various colors of construction paper

Preparation: None

Lesson:
1. Ask your child if snow is white. Ask them if the snow melts will it still be white?
2. Go outside with your child and gather some snow (you can play outside with them for awhile before coming back inside.) ☺
3. *NOTE: If you live in a warmer climate, you can try shaving some ice and asking your child this same question.*
4. Let your child test out their theory by letting some snow melt and painting with it on various colors of paper.
5. Once they've figured out that melted snow is water, ask them how they think they could make the melted snow white.

Literature –
The popcorn shop by Alice Low
Angelina of Italy by Maya Angelou
Bob's pizza by Louisa Campbell
Curious George and the pizza by Margret Rey and Alan J. Shalleck

Lesson Seventy-Seven – Tuesday

English – Neat White Stuff

Materials: None

Preparation: None

Lesson:
1. Take a walk around the house with your child.
2. Ask them to point out white objects that they think are really neat.

Pre-Math – Pepperoni Pizza

Materials: Pre-Made pizza crust (or you can make it from scratch)
               Pepperoni
               Whatever else you want on your pizza (sauce, mozzarella cheese, etc.)

Preparation: None

Lesson:
1. Let your child help you to make the pizza.
2. Be sure to let them count out 8 pepperonis to put on the pizza.
3. You and your child can enjoy the pizza for lunch.

Art – Chalk Drawing

Materials: White chalk
               Black construction paper

Preparation: None

Lesson: Let your child make a chalk drawing on the black construction paper.

Fine Motor Skills – Pizza Sauce Painting

Materials: Pizza sauce
               Paper

Preparation: None

Lesson: Let your child paint a picture with the pizza sauce. For a neat sensory art
               project, let them finger paint!

Literature -
<u>Detective Dan and the puzzling pizza mystery</u> by Timothy Roland
<u>Dinosaur pizza</u> by Lee Wardlaw
<u>Huggly's pizza</u> by Tedd Arnold
<u>The king of pizza : a magical story about the world's favorite food</u> by Sylvester Sanzari

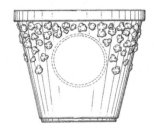

Lesson Seventy-Eight – Wednesday

English – P Tongue Twisters

Materials: None

Preparation: None

Lesson:
1. Practice some tongue twisters with your child:
   a. "Peter Piper picked a peck of pickled peppers. How many pickled peppers did Peter Piper pick?"
2. Let your child come up with a new P tongue twister of their own. Anything goes, real words or pretend words – as long as they all start with the letter P.

Pre-Math – Sorting

Materials: Polka-dot fabric squares or colored pom-poms

Preparation: None

Lesson: Put the fabric or the pom-poms in front of your child and let them sort by pattern or color.

Art - Popcorn Shake

Materials: Popped popcorn
               Paint
               A bag
               Construction paper
               Glue

Preparation: None

Lesson:
1. Let your child put the popcorn into the bag.
2. Have your child drizzle some paint into the bag and shake it.
3. After the paint dries, let your child glue their popcorn onto the paper to make a fun design.

Gross Motor Skills – Pizza Box

Materials: 2 empty pizza boxes

Preparation: Cut holes in the top of the pizza boxes big enough for your child to put
               their feet in them.

Lesson:
1. Have your child put the pizza boxes on their feet like shoes.
2. Do a relay with your child shuffling across the floor.

Science – Changing Colors

Materials: Darker color of paint
               White paint
               Paper (optional)

Preparation: None

Lesson:
1. Show your child how adding white paint to a darker color will make the dark
   color lighter.
2. You can let your child paint a picture with the paint afterwards if you would like.

Literature -
One pizza, one penny by K.T. Hao
Fox in socks by Dr. Seuss
She sells seashells : a tongue twister story by Grace Kim
Six thick thumbs : a tongue-twisting tale by Steve Charney

Lesson Seventy-Nine – Thursday

English – Prince or Princess Crown

Materials: Yellow construction paper
               Crayons
               Beads or fake jewels (optional)
               Tape or stapler

Preparation: Cut a crown shape out of the construction paper.

Lesson:
1. Let your child decorate their crown.
2. Help them to write their name on their crown. If they need help with this skill, write their name with yellow marker and let your child trace it.
3. Fasten the crown around your child's head and let them be a prince or a princess for the day.

Pre-Math – Count the Peas

Materials: Dried peas
               2 bowls

Preparation: None

Lesson:
1. Put varying amounts of peas into one bowl.
2. Have your child count them as they move them from one bowl to the next.
3. Do this several times with different amounts of peas.

Music – Feel the Beat

Materials: A variety of music CDs (classical, country, pop, etc.)
               Paper
               Paint or crayons

Preparation: None

Lesson:
1. Put in different types of music for your child to listen to.
2. Give your child a piece of paper and some paint or crayons.
3. Have them draw or paint at the speed and with the feeling of whatever music they are listening to at the time.
4. This is a great way to show your child how different types of music make us feel differently.

Fine Motor Skills – Pizza Play-Doh

Materials: Play-Doh
                Plastic pizza cutter (from a Play-Doh or child's cooking set)

Preparation: None

Lesson:
1. Show your child how to make lines up, down and across with a plastic pizza cutter.
2. Let your child practice.

Science – What Does White Feel Like?

Materials: Mashed potatoes
                Cool Whip
                Hard boiled egg

Preparation: None

Lesson:
1. Let your child compare the look, feel, and taste of these white foods.
2. You can also try sprinkling salt or sugar on these items to see which foods taste good with which.

Literature -
Mrs. Hippo's Pizza Parlour by Vivian French
Ord eats a pizza! by Irene Trimble
Pete's a pizza by William Steig
Pizza at Sally's by Monica Wellington

Lesson Eighty – Friday

English – Hide the P

Materials: Construction paper

Preparation: Cut a capital P out of the construction paper.

Lesson:
1. Hide the letter somewhere close to an object in your house which begins with the letter P.
2. Let your child look for the letter.
3. You can either say "warmer" or "colder" as they get close – or you can clap faster or slower as they get close.
4. Do this activity several times – either hide the P out in the open or slightly hidden depending on your child's ability.

Pre-Math – Popcorn Count

Materials: Paper plates
                Popped popcorn

Preparation: Write different numbers on the paper plates.

Lesson:
1. Have your child put the correct number of popcorn pieces onto each plate. Try to let them identify the numbers on their own if they are able.
2. Then tell your child they can eat the pile of 3, of 4, etc.

Art – Popcorn Collage

Materials: Glue
                Food coloring or paint
                Paper
                Popcorn

Preparation: Mix the paint or the food coloring with the glue to color it.

Lesson:
1. Provide your child with many different colors of glue.
2. Let your child paint a picture with the glue – be sure the glue is thick enough to hold the popcorn on the page.
3. Let your child press the popcorn onto the painted parts.

Gross Motor Skills – Air Popping Corn

Materials: Air popper
                Unpopped popcorn
                Small bucket or cup

Preparation: None

Lesson:
1. Put the air popper in the middle of the floor – do NOT put the lid on it.
2. Have your child stand back as you turn it on and it heats up.
3. As the popcorn starts popping and flying out, let your child try to catch some of the popcorn in their bucket.
4. This makes a big mess but is SO MUCH FUN for your child.

Science – Individual Pizzas

Materials: English muffins or Ritz crackers
                Pizza sauce
                Mozzarella cheese

Preparation: None

Lesson:
1. Let your child make their own individual pizza.
2. Bake the pizzas until the cheese melts and let your child enjoy it for a snack or for lunch.

Literature -
Pizza Pat by Rita Goldman Gelman
The pizza that we made by Joan Holub
Ricky, Rocky, and Ringo count on pizza by Mauri Kunnas
Shanna's pizza parlor by Jean Marzollo

Week Seventeen

Your theme for this week will be *quilts*. You will be focusing on the following topics with your child:

English – The letter Q
Pre-Math – Rectangles and the number 9
Art – The color black

Lesson Eighty-One – Monday

English: Recognition of the Letter Q

Materials: Card stock
              Various colors of construction paper
              Glue stick

Preparation:
1. Cut a capital letter Q out of card stock.
2. Cut squares out of different colors of construction paper.

Lesson: Let your child glue the different-colored squares onto their Q so that it looks like a quilt.

Pre-Math – Snack People

Materials: Round crackers
              Rectangle crackers
              Peanut butter
              Raisins
              Plastic knife or cheese spreader

Preparation: None

Lesson:
1. Let your child spread peanut butter a round cracker (the head) and a rectangular cracker (the body) and put them together on a plate.
2. Have them count out 9 raisins to use for creating the face and buttons on the person's shirt.
3. Let your child eat their Snack People.

Art – Create a Quilt

Materials: Construction paper
                  A real quilt (or a picture of a quilt)
                  Several colorful fabrics
                  Glue

Preparation:
1. Fold the construction paper into several squares.
2. Cut squares of the same size from the fabrics.

Lesson:
1. Show your child the quilt.
2. Let your child choose fabric squares and glue them onto their papers to make their own quilt.

Gross Motor Skills – Hopscotch

Materials: Orange, black and yellow construction paper

Preparation: Tape the construction paper onto the floor in a hopscotch pattern.

Lesson: Allow your child to go through stepping on only one color, then the next, and then the last.

Literature -
The bone talker by Shelley A. Leedahl
The dream quilt by Celeste Ryan
A far-fetched story by Karin Cates
Grandpa's quilt by Betsy Franco

Lesson Eighty-Two – Tuesday

English – Neat Black Stuff

Materials: None

Preparation: None

Lesson:
1. Take a walk around the house with your child.
2. Ask them to point out black objects that they think are really neat.

Pre-Math – Clouds in the Sky

Materials: White paper
                Blue paper
                Glue stick

Preparation: None

Lesson:
1. Have your child tear their white paper into 9 pieces to be the clouds.
2. Let your child glue their clouds onto the blue paper (the sky).

Fine Motor Skills – Quilts

Materials: Fabric scraps
                Carpet sample
                Hot glue gun
                Velcro

Preparation:
1. Cut the fabric scraps into different sizes of squares and triangles.
2. Hot glue small pieces of Velcro to the back of the fabric shapes.

Lesson:
1. Let your child make their own quilt patterns on top of the carpet sample.
2. This is great for their fine motor skills – and your child will love the unique quilt that they will make.

Literature –
I'm going to Grandma's by Mary Ann Hoberman
The keeping quilt by Patricia Polacco
Luka's quilt by Georgia Guback
The moon quilt by Sunny Warner

Lesson Eighty-Three – Wednesday

English – Visit Q-Land

Materials: Globe or map
Book or DVD about a place which begins with Q
Foods from a place which begins with Q (optional)
Paper
Crayons

Preparation: None

Lesson:
1. Go on a pretend trip to somewhere that begins with the letter Q (i.e., Queensland, Australia; Qatar; Quantico; Queens, New York; Quebec, Canada; etc.)
2. Find the location on the map or globe.
3. Pretend to fly or drive to your location.
4. (optional) Let your child sample some food from your location.
5. Talk to your child about what people are like, how they dress, how they behave, etc.
6. Watch a DVD or read a book about your location.
7. Have your child dictate and illustrate a story about their "trip."

Pre-Math – Quarters and Other Money

Materials: A Penny
A Nickel
A Dime
A Quarter
A One Dollar bill

Preparation: None

Lesson:
1. Show your child each piece of money. Point out its color, shape, size, pictures and writing on each side, etc.
2. Show your child the number on each coin or bill and tell them how much it's worth.
3. Be patient with your child. Remember that you are just introducing these concepts and they aren't going to fully understand everything at this point.

Art – Q-Tip Painting

Materials: Q-tips
                Paint
                Paper

Preparation: None

Lesson: Let your child paint with Q-Tips.

Fine Motor Skills – Paint the House

Materials: Water
                Bowl or bucket
                Paintbrush

Preparation: None

Lesson: Let your child paint different items in your house with the water – whatever you'd like that isn't going to be hurt by having water on it (i.e., the refrigerator, the kitchen floor, the counter, etc.)

Literature -
The name quilt by Phyllis Root
Papa and the pioneer quilt by Jean Van Leeuwen
The patchwork path : a quilt map to freedom by Bettye Stroud
Peter's patchwork dream by Willemien Min

Lesson Eighty-Four – Thursday

English – Black Animal Sort

Materials: Old magazines or newspaper inserts
                    Scissors
                    Paper (optional)
                    Glue Stick (optional)

Preparation: None

Lesson:
1. Let your child look through some old magazines and cut out pictures of black animals.
2. Have your child sort the animals by whether they have black skin, black fur or black feathers.
3. Optionally, you can have your child make a book or a collage of their findings.

Pre-Math – Quarter Sort

Materials: A pile of change (including dimes, nickels, pennies, and quarters)

Preparation: None

Lesson:
1. Ask your child to show you a coin with a 10 on it, a 5 on it, etc.
2. Put a bunch of coins on the table and ask your child to help you sort them.
3. The more they do this activity the faster they will be able to easily identify and sort the coins.

Music – Dance and Play

Materials: <u>Laugh A Little: 15 Silly Songs for Little Ones</u> or other music CD

Preparation: None

Lesson:
1. Dance to the music with your child.
2. The goofier you are willing to get, the more fun you and your child will have together.

Fine Motor Skills – The Cutting Pail

Materials: Paper (can be scrap paper)
                Scissors
                An empty pail

Preparation: None

Lesson: Let your child cut up the paper however they would like and put the pieces into the pail. You can save these pieces of paper and use them later for different lessons.

Literature -
Quilt counting by Lesa Cline-Ransome
A quilt for baby by Kim Lewis
Reuben and the quilt by P. Buckley Moss
The secret to freedom by Marcia Vaughan

Lesson Eighty-Five – Friday

English – Alphabetical Order

Materials: A-Q Flashcards

Preparation: None

Lesson:
1. Let your child try to put the flashcards in alphabetical order.
2. Mix them up and have them try it again. Let them continue until they can do it quickly without struggling.

Pre-Math – Coins By Feel

Materials: A handful of coins
               An empty purse

Preparation: None

Lesson:
1. Drop a coin into the purse.
2. Let your child feel inside the purse and see if they can tell which coin it is simply by feeling it.
3. Do this several times with different coins.

Art – Quivers

Materials: Empty paper towel roll
               Crayons or markers
               Paper
               Yarn
               Pipe cleaners
               Foam (optional)

Preparation: None

Lesson:
1. Let your child decorate their paper towel roll.
2. Help your child attach the yarn for a strap.
3. Make arrows out of pipe cleaners. Make the tips and ends from foam or paper.

Gross Motor Skills – Wash the Windows

Materials: Squirt bottle with window cleaner
              Paper towels or a cloth

Preparation: None

Lesson:
1. Give your child the squirt bottle and the towels and let him or her go to town.
2. This is great for their gross motor skills and it will keep them entertained for hours!

Literature -
Bruno the tailor by Lars Klinting
The log cabin quilt by Ellen Howard
Down Buttermilk Lane by Barbara Mitchell
Just plain fancy by Patricia Polacco

Week Eighteen

Your theme for this week will be *rainbows*. You will be focusing on the following topics with your child:

English – The letter R
Pre-Math – Arc and the number 9
Art – The colors of the rainbow (red, orange, yellow, green, blue, indigo, violet)

Lesson Eighty-Six – Monday

English: Recognition of the Letter R

Materials: Card stock
                Paint or markers

Preparation: Cut a capital letter R out of card stock.

Lesson: Let your child either color or paint their R to look like a rainbow.

Art – Rainy Day Picture

Materials: Cotton balls
                Blue construction paper
                White construction paper
                Aluminum foil
                Glue stick

Preparation:
1. Cut rain drops out of the blue construction paper.
2. Cut lightning and rain puddles out of the aluminum foil.

Lesson:
1. Have your child make a rainy day picture.
    a. Let them make clouds with the cotton balls.
    b. Have them glue on several raindrops.
    c. Have them glue on the lightning bolts and the rain puddles.
2. This picture will be used for today's math lesson.

Pre-Math – Count the Raindrops

Materials: Rainy Day Picture from Art Lesson

Preparation: None

Lesson: Help your child to count the raindrops on their picture. They can count
              the other elements on their picture as well.

Gross Motor Skills – Watch Out for Puddles

Materials: Blue construction paper
              Tape (optional)

Preparation: Cut out several rain puddles from the construction paper.

Lesson:
1. Scatter the puddles around on the floor. You can tape them to the floor if you
   would like.
2. Have your child try to jump over the puddles without getting "wet."

Science – Rainbow Bottle

Materials: Liquid with different densities (i.e., oil, water, alcohol)
              Food coloring
              Clear bottle w/ a top

Preparation: Use food coloring to die each liquid a different color.

Lesson:
1. Put the liquids in the bottle (first the oil, then the water, then the alcohol).
2. Secure the lid with a top.
3. Let your child turn the bottle upside down and watch the liquids mix and un-mix.
   Let your child play with the bottle and observe the colors.

Literature -
On Noah's Ark by Jan Brett
Ned's rainbow by Melanie Walsh
The rainbow mystery by Jennifer Dussling
What makes a rainbow? by Betty Ann Schwartz

Lesson Eighty-Seven – Tuesday

English – Planting a Rainbow

Materials: <u>Planting a Rainbow</u> by Lois Ehlert

Preparation: None

Lesson: Read and discuss the book with your child.

Pre-Math – Fruit Loop Rainbow

Materials: Large piece of paper or poster board
               Box of Fruit Loops cereal
               Glue (optional)

Preparation:
1. Draw a large rainbow on the paper.
2. Color in the bows of the rainbow (from top to bottom = red, orange, yellow, green, blue, indigo, violet – it's all right if you skip the indigo bow)

Lesson:
1. Let your child sort and match the fruit loops to the correct bow of the rainbow.
2. Optionally, you can let your child glue the cereal in place. Otherwise they can eat the cereal (or some of it) when they are done.

Fine Motor Skills – Rainbow Game

Materials: None

Preparation: Be sure there are regular household items throughout the house of all colors of the rainbow.

Lesson:
1. Ask your child to look around the house and collect red objects. Put them in a pile.
2. Repeat this with orange, yellow, green, blue, and purple.
3. Help your child to arrange the objects on the floor into a rainbow shape, in the proper order in which they appear in a rainbow.

Science – Color Mixing Activity

Materials: Red, yellow, and blue finger paints
               3 Paper plates
               Wet paper towels

Preparation: None

Lesson:
1. On the paper plates, let your child mix together the different primary colors of finger paints with each other to form the secondary colors of orange, green, and purple.
2. Provide wet paper towels so your child can clean their fingers between colors.

Literature -
Patrick paints a picture by Saviour Pirotta
Colors by Gillian Youldon
Carl's nose by Karen Lee Schmidt
Cloudy with a chance of meatballs by Judi Barrett

Lesson Eighty-Eight – Wednesday

English – Catching a Rainbow

Materials: Clear glass or medium-sized jar
Window sill
White paper
Watercolor paints or crayons

Preparation: It must be a bright, sunny day for this to work!

Lesson:
1. Fill the glass or jar to the top with water.
2. Set the glass on a window sill on a bright, sunny day.
3. The glass or jar should stick out over the ledge a little bit.
4. Place the paper on the floor in front of the window.
5. Help your child move the jar from side to side on the window sill until a rainbow is reflected on the paper. Tell your child that they caught the rainbow!
6. Draw lines to capture the rainbow and let your child paint or color the bows of the rainbow.

Pre-Math – Spinning Colors

Materials: Heavy paper
Sharpened pencil

Preparation:
1. Cut a circle out of the paper.
2. Divide the paper into 6 equal sections. Color each section a different color of the rainbow.
3. Poke a sharpened pencil through the center of the circle.

Lesson:
1. Ask your child to guess what they will see when you spin the disk.
2. When the disk spins, you should see white – or close to white – depending on how true the colors are and how equal the sections are.
3. Explain to your child that this is the opposite of how a rainbow is created. In a rainbow, white light is separated into 6 colors. In this experiment, 6 colors are spun together to make white.

Art – Rainbow Sticks

Materials: Empty paper towel roll
                     Masking tape
                     Glue
                     Paint
                     Uncooked rice
                     Toothpicks

Preparation: Poke lots of holes through both sides of the paper towel roll.

Lesson:
1. Have your child poke the toothpicks through the holes so that they go in one side and out the other.
2. Glue both ends of the toothpicks.
3. Help your child to tape one end of the roll closed.
4. Help your child to pour some rice in the other end of the roll.
5. Let your child paint their sticks like a rainbow.
6. After the paint dries, cut off any toothpick ends which are sticking out.
7. Let your child tip the stick back and forth – it will sound like the rain.

Fine Motor Skills – Lacing Rainbows

Materials: Picture of a rainbow (see companion download)
                     Poster board
                     Thin shoestring
                     Hole puncher
                     Contact paper (optional)

Preparation:
1. Print the rainbow from the companion download onto a piece of poster board.
2. Laminate the rainbow or cover it with contact paper to make it more durable.
3. Use the hole puncher to punch holes around the edges of the rainbow.
4. Tie the shoestring to one of the holes

Lesson:
1. Give your child the rainbow and string.
2. Show them how to lace the rainbow.
3. This is great for developing their fine motor skills.
4. Let them lace and unlace the rainbow as many times as they are willing.

Science – Different Shades of Rainbow Colors

Materials: White ice cube tray
                  Red, yellow and blue food coloring
                  Eye dropper or medicine dropper

Preparation: Fill the first 3 holes in the tray with red water, yellow water and blue water.

Lesson:
1. Give your child the eye dropper and let them mix the colors in the empty spaces of the ice cube tray. This will allow them to create many different shades of colors.
2. Once the ice cubes have hardened, let your child add their colored ice cubes to a drink – or play with them – whichever you prefer.

Literature -
Take a walk on a rainbow : a first look at color by Miriam Moss
It's raining, it's pouring by Kin Eagle
Splosh! by Mick Inkpen
Sammy's secret by Margaret Nash

Lesson Eighty-Nine – Thursday

English – Noah's Rainbow

Materials: Two by Two: The Story of Noah's Faith by Marilyn
               Lashbrook

Preparation: None

Lesson:
1. Read the book about Noah's Ark.
2. Discuss with your child who made the rainbow and why.

Pre-Math – Colorful Necklace

Materials: Fruit Loops cereal
               String

Preparation: None

Lesson:
1. Let your child sort the cereal into separate colors.
2. Have them string the cereal onto the string.
3. Help your child to fasten their string into a necklace.
4. Let your child eat the cereal off of their necklace throughout the day.

Gross Motor Skills – Animal Acting

Materials: None

Preparation: None

Lesson:
1. Have your child act like different animals that are headed to Noah's ark.
   a. Have them walk like a cow (crawl on all fours).
   b. Have them slither like a snake.
   c. Have them do the crab walk.
   d. Have them gallop like a horse, etc.

Science – Gelatin Rainbow Snack

Materials: Clear plastic cups
              Six colors of Jello – cherry, orange, lemon, lime, berry blue, and grape.
              Cool Whip

Preparation:
   1. Make all six colors of Jello in separate containers.
   2. After the Jello has set, spoon one spoonful of each color into a clear cup.
   3. Top with a "cloud" of cool whip.

Lesson:
   1. Let your child eat their edible rainbow.
   2. Ask them to identify whatever color is on their spoon as they take bites.

Literature –
Noah's Ark by Lisbeth Zwerger
The Searcher and Old Tree by David McPhail
When rain falls by Melissa Stewart
Who likes the rain? by written by Etta Kaner

Lesson Ninety – Friday

English – My Rainbow Book

Materials: Old magazines or newspaper inserts
                  Construction paper
                  Stapler
                  Glue Stick
                  Scissors

Preparation: Fold and staple the construction paper into a book with 6 pages.

Lesson:
1. Let your child look through the old magazines to find pictures of objects that are all different colors.
2. Have your child make a rainbow book by gluing items onto a red page, a orange page, a blue page, etc.

Pre-Math – Multi-color Binoculars

Materials: 2 Empty toilet paper rolls
                  2 Rubber bands
                  Colored plastic wrap

Preparation: Cut the plastic wrap into 4 x 4 inch squares.

Lesson:
1. Help your child to place a colored square evenly over the end of one of the toilet paper rolls.
2. While holding the square in place, put a rubber band over it to secure it.
3. Repeat with the other toilet paper roll.
4. Watch as your child explores the world around them in the color whatever color you have chosen. You may want to let them try several different colors.

Art – Cloud Paintings

Materials: Shaving cream
                  Glue
                  Construction paper

Preparation: Mix together the shaving cream and glue in equal parts.

Lesson: Let your child finger paint with the mixture.

Fine Motor Skills – Drawing Circles

Materials: Paper
                Crayons
                Yellow highlighter (optional)

Preparation: None

Lesson:
1. Give your child some paper and crayons.
2. Instruct them to practice drawing circles on their paper.
3. If they are struggling with this skill, draw some circles on the paper with the yellow highlighter and let your child trace them.
4. Once they feel comfortable, they can try to draw some circles on their own.

Science – Colorful Toast

Materials: Milk
                Food coloring
                Bowls

Preparation: Pour the milk into the bowls and add different colors of food coloring to each bowl. Mix them together.

Lesson:
1. Let your child paint the bread with the colored milk.
2. When they are done, you can toast the bread as you usually would.
3. Let them eat their colorful toast.

Literature -
Cloud boy by Rhode Montijo
Ken's cloud by Isabel M. Arques
Little cloud by Eric Carle
The police cloud by Christoph Niemann

Week Nineteen

Your theme for this week will be the *sky and the stars*. You will be focusing on the following topics with your child:

English – The letter S
Pre-Math – Circles and the number 10
Art – The color white

Lesson Ninety-One – Monday

English: Recognition of the Letter S

Materials: Card stock
                Star stickers

Preparation: Cut a capital letter S out of card stock.

Lesson: Let your child stick the star stickers all over their capital S.

Pre-Math – Count to Ten

Materials: Paper lunch bag
                Small objects you have ten of in your house (i.e., crayons, markers,
                    counters, pegs, craft sticks, etc.)

Preparation: Put one of each small object in the lunch bag.

Lesson:
1. Have your child pull one item out of their bag.
2. Let your child look around the house and bring 10 matching items back to you.
    Be sure your child counts out the objects.

Art – Create a Constellation

Materials: Black construction paper
Star stickers
White chalk (optional)

Preparation: None

Lesson:
1. Let your child arrange the star stickers on their paper however they would like to make up some constellations.
2. (Optional) Using the white chalk, you have your child connect the "dots" on their paper to draw out their constellations.
3. (Optional) Have your child name their constellations.

Gross Motor Skills – Astronaut Exercise

Materials: None

Preparation: None

Lesson:
1. Talk to your children about how they're going to pretend to be an astronaut. Tell them that astronauts need to be in top physical condition to be able to endure traveling through space.
2. Do the following exercises with your little astronauts in training:
   a. **Solar System Stretch** – Have your child reach to the sky, then stretch arms out wide.
   b. **Rocket Run** – Have your child run in place as they get ready to take off.
   c. **Galaxy Gallop** – Have your child gallop around the galaxy (your living room).
   d. **Lunar Leap** – Have your child do a standing long jump.
   e. **Trainee Toe Touches** – Have your child touch their toes 10 times.
   f. **Planet Push-Ups** – Have your child do 8 or 9 push-ups – one for each planet (depending on whether or not you consider Pluto a planet.)
   g. **Constellation Cool Down** – Lie on your back with your child. Help them to imagine staring up at a starry sky while they relax from their exercise.

Science – The Solar System

Materials: Styrofoam balls
                    Paint
                    Various art supplies

Preparation: None

Lesson:
1. You and your child can design your own planets.
2. After they have all dried, you can put them together to be a solar system.

Literature -
How to catch a star by Oliver Jeffers
Night goes by by Kate Spohn
Shine! by Karen and Jonathan Langley
Thomas and the shooting star by Tommy Stubbs

Lesson Ninety-Two – Tuesday

English – Play-Doh Shapes

Materials: Play-Doh
                     Cookie cutters - S and stars (optional)
                     Plastic knife

Preparation: None

Lesson: Let your child cut S shapes and star shapes out of the Play-Doh.

Pre-Math – Numerical Order

Materials: 1-10 Flashcards

Preparation: None

Lesson:
1. Let your child try to put the flashcards in numerical order.
2. Mix them up and have them try it again. Let them continue until they can do it quickly without struggling.

Fine Motor – Astronaut Food

Materials: Package of instant pudding
                     Milk (see back of pudding package for amount)
                     Ziploc bag

Preparation: None

Lesson:
1. Help your child to pour about ¼ of the instant pudding into a baggie.
2. Help your child to pour ¼ of the recommended amount of milk into the baggie.
3. Seal the bag securely for your child.
4. Let your child squeeze and shake their bag until it starts to thicken.
5. Put the baggie in the refrigerator for an hour.
6. Cut off one of the corners of the baggie and let your child eat the pudding by sucking it through the hole.

Literature -
Above us, in the sky by Eric Carle
Mommy's little star by Janet Bingham
What is in the sky? by Cindy Chapman
I am a star by Jean Marzollo

Lesson Ninety-Three – Wednesday

English – S is for Smile

Materials: Smiley face stickers
               Paper

Preparation: Draw a large S on the paper.

Lesson: Let your child stick the stickers along the outline of their letter S.

Pre-Math – How Many Stars?

Materials: Index cards
               Crayons or markers

Preparation: Write the numbers 1-10 on separate index cards.

Lesson:
   1. Ask your child to draw the correct number of stars indicated on each of the index cards.
   2. If your child gets frustrated trying to draw a star, let them draw circles or even dots instead.

Art – Spray Bottle Solar System

Materials: White paint
               Spray bottle
               Black construction paper
               Crayons or markers
               Various art supplies
               Newspapers
               Solar system pictures (search for some on the internet)

Preparation: Dilute some white paint with water and put it into the spray bottle.

Lesson:
   1. Protect your working area with newspapers.
   2. Show your child the solar system pictures.
   3. Let your child spray the paint mixture onto their black paper. This will make the paper look like space. Let your child design their own solar system on their paper.

Gross Motor Skills – Moon Rock Throw

Materials: Sheets of scrap paper
               Laundry basket

Preparation: None

Lesson:
1. Help your child to wad up some scrap paper into moon rock shapes.
2. Let your child try to throw the "moon rocks" into the laundry basket.

Science – Balloon Rocket

Materials: String
               Straw
               Long balloon
               Tape

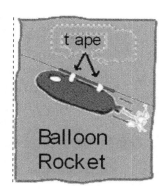

Preparation:
1. Tie one end of the string to a chair, door knob, or other support.
2. Put the other end of the string through the straw.
3. Pull the string tight and tie it to another support across the room.

Lesson:
3. Blow up the balloon (but don't tie it).
4. Pinch the end of the balloon and tape it to the straw. You're ready to launch your rocket.
5. Let go and watch the rocket fly!

Literature -
I like stars by Margaret Wise Brown
Our stars by Anne Rockwell
Twinkle by Jane and Ann Taylor
Twinkle, twinkle little star by Jane Taylor

Lesson Ninety-Four – Thursday

English: Play Hide the S

Materials: White card stock or construction paper

Preparation: Cut a large capital and a large lowercase
letter S out of the card stock or
construction paper.

Lesson:
1. Hide the letters somewhere. Begin by hiding the letters out in the open, then slightly camouflage them if your child's ability allows.
2. Try to put the letters near objects which begin with the letter S.
3. Talk to your child about the sounds that the letter S makes.
4. Let your child look for the letters. Tell them if they're getting warmer if they get closer or colder if they get farther away.
5. After they find the letters, see if they can identify the object near the letter which begins with the letter S.

Pre-Math – Number Recognition Hoops

Materials: 0-10 Flashcards
Several hula hoops – or use masking tape to make circles on the floor
Child's Music CD (optional)

Preparation: None

Lesson:
1. Place several of the numbers inside the hoops.
2. Play some music or have your child sing and dance around the hoops.
3. When a song is done, call out a number.
4. Your child should find hoop containing the number you have called out and jump inside that hoop.
5. Do this several times with different numbers.

Music – 1, 2, Buckle My Shoe

Materials: None

Preparation: None

Lesson: Sing the rhyme with your child:

1, 2, Buckle my shoe
3, 4, Shut the door
5, 6, Pickup sticks
7, 8, Lay them straight
9, 10, A BIG FAT HEN!

Fine Motor Skills – Lite Brite Constellations

Materials: A Lite Brite
Blank Lite Brite page

Preparation: None

Lesson:
1. Plug in the Lite Brite so that the light is on.
2. Let your child stick in the pegs to create their own constellations.

Literature -
Cold Night, Brittle Light by Richard Thompson
Harold's Trip to the Sky by Crockett Johnson
Like Butter on Pancakes by Jonathan London
Hello Sun! by Hans Wilhelm

Lesson Ninety-Five – Friday

English – Tracing an S

Materials: Card stock
                   Paper
                   Pencil

Preparation: Write the letter S on the card stock.

Lesson:
1. Put the paper over the card with the letter S.
2. Let your child trace the S with a pencil.
3. An alternative way to do this is to tape the card and the paper to a window on a sunny day and let your child trace the S that way.

Pre-Math – Ten Eggs

Materials: 10 Plastic eggs
                   Empty egg carton

Preparation: Cut 2 of the sections off of the egg carton.

Lesson:
1. Give your child the 10 eggs.
2. Have your child place the eggs into the egg carton.
3. Your child will be using 1 to 1 correspondence when they do this activity.

Art – Telescope

Materials: Empty paper towel tube
                   Paint
                   Black tissue paper
                   Various art supplies
                   Paperclip

Preparation: None

Lesson:
1. Help your child put two pieces of black tissue paper at one end of a paper towel tube and fasten them with a rubber band.
2. Using the end of the paperclip, carefully punch several small holes in the tissue paper.
3. Let your child decorate their telescope however they would like.
4. Once the paint has dried, let your child look through their telescope. When they hold it up to a light, they will see stars.

Gross Motor Skills – Fun With S

Materials: Rolled sock
                      Rope

Preparation: None

Lesson:
1. **Fun Activity #1** - Have your child toss a rolled sock into the air and then catch it. Let them do this repeatedly.
2. **Fun Activity #2** – Wiggle a rope on the floor and have your child try to jump over the "snake" without touching it.

Science – Rocket Launch

Materials: Alka-Seltzer tablet
                      Empty 35mm film cartridge w/ lid

Preparation: None

Lesson:
1. Place the Alka-Seltzer tablet and a little bit of water in the 35mm film cartridge.
2. Close the cartridge lid tightly.
3. Place the cartridge on the floor and stand back.
4. Very soon, the top will launch about chest high – the pressure from the gas causes the lid to pop off and fly up.

Literature -
Space Case by Edward Marshall
Countdown! by Kay Woodward
Man on the moon : a day in the life of Bob by Simon Bartram
Max paints the house by Ken Wilson-Max

Week Twenty

Your theme for this week will be *transportation*. You will be focusing on the following topics with your child:

English – The letter T
Pre-Math – Rectangles and the number 10
Art – The color orange

Lesson Ninety-Six – Monday

English: Recognition of the Letter T

Materials: Card stock
                Toothpicks
                Glue

Preparation: Cut a capital letter T out of card stock.

Lesson: Let your child glue toothpicks all over their letter T.

Pre-Math – Telephone Pole Count

Materials: None

Preparation: None

Lesson: Take a trip in the car. Let your child count the telephone poles as you pass them. This helps your child to practice counting as well as to give them a sense of time and space.

Art – Train Whistle

Materials: Empty toilet paper tube
                Paint
                Hole punch
                Wax paper
                Rubber band

Preparation: None

Lesson:
1. Let your child decorate the toilet paper tube with paint.
2. Once the paint is dry, punch a hole about half an inch down the tube.
3. Put a circle of wax paper over one end of the tube and secure it with a rubber band.
4. Let your child pretend to be a train with their train whistle. (It will actually sound more like a kazoo.)

Gross Motor Skills – Red Light, Green Light

Materials: Red constructionpPaper
                Green construction paper

Preparation: Cut out a green circle and a red circle.

Lesson:
1. Play the classic game of Red Light, Green Light.
2. When you hold up the green circle, your child can run toward you.
3. When you hold up the red circle they must stop.

Science – My Airplane

Materials: Empty paper towel tube
                Cardboard or card stock
                Paint
                Markers or crayons
                Various art supplies

Preparation: Cut a slit all the way through the paper towel roll. Draw airplane wings on the cardboard or card stock.

Lesson:
1. Let your child cut out their airplane wings if they are able.
2. Help your child to stick the wings in the slit.
3. Let your child decorate their own airplane.

Literature –
All things that go by Dandi
Choo choo clickety-clack! by Margaret Mayo
From Kalamazoo to Timbuktu! by Harriet Ziefert
Bunnies on the go : getting from place to place by Rick Walton

Lesson Ninety-Seven – Tuesday

English – What's In Your Suitcase?

Materials: None

Preparation: None

Lesson:
1. Go back and forth with your child and say this phrase: "I'm going on a trip and I'm going to put _____ in my suitcase." Fill in the blank with an item which starts with the letter T.
2. Another variation you can play would be to start with an item that begins with A and work your way through the alphabet (i.e., A = apple, B = blow dryer, etc.)

Pre-Math – Shape Train

Materials: At least 8 blocks of 2 different shapes

Preparation: None

Lesson:
1. Discuss which shapes the blocks are with your child.
2. Let your child examine and touch the differently shaped blocks.
3. Tell your child you're going to build a shape train.
4. Lay down 6 blocks in a row, alternating shapes.
5. To help your child understand the pattern, point to each block and ask them which shapes they are. Talk about the pattern with them.
6. Ask your child to add the next block and to tell you why they chose the shape they chose.
7. Have your child continue adding blocks according to the pattern.

Geography – My Map

Materials: Various maps
                      Paper
                      Crayons or markers
                      Paint
                      Various art supplies of your choice

Preparation: None

Lesson:
1. Show your child several maps – possibly of their city, their state, their country, etc.
2. Let your child design a map of their own. This can either be a realistic map or a map of a pretend place, whichever they would prefer.

Fine Motor Skills – My Construction Site

Materials: Gravel or sand
                      Several small rocks or pebbles
                      Construction truck toys
                      Large bucket or bin

Preparation: Fill the bucket or bin with the gravel or sand.

Lesson: Let your child play with the construction trucks. Have them use the trucks to move the rocks around.

Science – Train Whistle

Materials: Empty 2-liter bottle

Preparation: None

Lesson:
1. Talk to your child about how trains have different whistle patterns they use when they are crossing a road, passing another train, etc.
2. Show your child how to blow across the top of the empty bottle to get a whistling sound.
3. Let your child practice blowing across the top of the bottle.

Literature –
Cars! cars! cars! by Grace Maccarone
Go Bugs Go! by Jessica Spanyol
Going to Grandma's farm by Betsy Franco
Heidi's hike by Jeffrey Sculthorp

Lesson Ninety-Eight – Wednesday

English – Word Matching

Materials: Paper
                Pictures of different modes of transportation
                    (see companion download)

Preparation: Print and cut out the transportation vehicles and words from the
                companion download.

Lesson:
   1. Give your child the cutouts.
   2. Help them to match the words to the correct vehicle. This exposes your child to
      some words.

Pre-Math – Stoplight Graph

Materials: Paper
                Stickers

Preparation:
   1. Make two columns on the paper.
   2. Write a red X at the top of one column and a green X at the top of the other.

Lesson:
   1. Go on a car ride with your child.
   2. Ask your child to put a sticker in the red column every time you stop at a red light
      and a sticker in the green column every time you go through a green light.
   3. Ask your child if there were more red lights or green lights.
   4. This exercise will help your child learn about recording and interpreting data and
      will learn that numbers can be relevant to their lives.

Art – Paper Airplanes

Materials: Paper

Preparation: None

Lesson: Let your child make paper airplanes and fly them.

Fine Motor Skills – Cutting Strips

Materials: Stiff paper with stripes (i.e., wallpaper samples)
                 Scissors

Preparation: None

Lesson:
1. Let your child cut along the stripes to make strips of paper.
2. After cutting the strips, let your child form the letter T with them.

Science – Ramps

Materials: Stiff paper, plastic or boards
                 Toy cars

Preparation: None

Lesson:
1. Help your child to make several ramps of different heights.
2. Let your child play with the cars on the ramps.
3. Ask your child which ramps make the cars go faster. See if they can tell you why.

Literature -
Here comes Grandma! by Janet Lord
I wish I were a pilot by Stella Blackstone
Red light, green light by Anastasia Suen
Six hogs on a scooter by Eileen Spinelli

Lesson Ninety-Nine – Thursday

English – Ticking Clock

Materials: None

Preparation: None

Lesson:
1. Tell your child that they can practice the sound of the letter T by repeating the sound of a ticking clock (t, t, t, t.)
2. You and your child pretend to be ticking clocks.

Pre-Math – License Plate Matching Game

Materials: Index cards
               Crayons or markers

Preparation: Make some pretend license plates to be used in a matching game.

Lesson: Have your child match the license plates by number, state, color, etc.

Music – Down by the Station

Materials: None

Preparation: None

Lesson: Sing the song "Down by the Station" with your child.

> ***Down By the Station***
> Down by the station
> Early in the morning
> See the little pufferbellies
> All in a row
> See the station master
> Turn the little handle
> Puff, puff, toot, toot
> Off we go!

Fine Motor Skills – Pin the Conductor on the Train

Materials: Conductor cutouts (see companion download)
                     Train cutout (see companion download)
                     Tape
                     Blindfold (optional)

Preparation: Print and cut out several copies of the conductor and one train.

Lesson:
1. Hang the train up on the wall about as high as your child's head.
2. Hand your child one of the conductors (with tape rolled up onto the back).
3. Put the blindfold on your child – or have them close their eyes.
4. Spin your child around several times.
5. Point your child toward the train and let them go. See how close they can get to putting their conductor on the train without using their other hand to feel around.

Science – Edible Traffic Lights

Materials: Graham crackers
                     Plastic knife or cheese spreader
                     Frosting or cream cheese
                     M&Ms

Preparation: None

Lesson:
1. Have your child break their graham cracker into rectangle-shaped pieces.
2. Let your child use the dull knife to spread the frosting or cream cheese on one of the rectangles.
3. Have your child put one red, one yellow, and one green M&M on their rectangle to be the "lights".
4. Let your child eat and enjoy their snack.

Literature -
Truck driver Tom by Monica Wellington
Wake up engines by Denise Dowling Mortensen
We all go traveling by Sheena Roberts
What James likes best by Amy Schwartz

Lesson One Hundred – Friday

English – Transportation Then and Now

Materials: Picture of car (see companion download)
Picture of covered wagon (see companion download)

Paper
Crayons

Preparation: Print the car and the covered wagon from the companion download.

Lesson:
1. Talk to your child about covered wagons that people used to use as compared to cars that we currently use.
2. Let your child color the pictures of the car and the covered wagon.

Pre-Math – Traffic Signs

Materials: Traffic sign pictures (see companion download)

Preparation: Print the traffic sign pictures from the companion download.

Lesson:
1. Tell your child that people communicate with symbols.
2. Talk to them about traffic signs – show them the pictures from the companion download.
3. Point out how the shape of the sign helps people to know what the sign says.
4. Point out the meaning of the different signs but don't push your child to remember them. You child will remember the meaning when they are ready.

Art – License Plate Rubbing

Materials: Old license plate
Paper
Crayons

Preparation: None

Lesson:
1. Have your child put the license plate underneath their paper. If you don't have an old license plate, they can take their paper out to your car and do this vertically.
2. Help your child to peel the paper off of one of their crayons.
3. Have your child hold their crayon on its side and rub it over the paper. The license plate will show up on the paper.

Fine Motor Skills – Toothpick Poke

Materials: Toothpicks
               Colander

Preparation: None

Lesson: Give your child some toothpicks and have him poke them through the
               holes in the colander – making it look like a porcupine.

Science – Balloon-Powered Car

Materials: Balloon
               Straw
               Tape
               Toy car

Preparation: Cut the lip off of the balloon. Cut the straw in half.

Lesson:
   1. Stick the straw into the balloon and tape it into place. Be sure to make a tight
      seal.
   2. Tape the straw to the top of the car so that the straw is off the back end.
   3. Blow up the balloon through the straw and seal the balloon by pinching the straw.
   4. Set the car down on a smooth surface and let it go.

Literature –
Going west adapted from the Little house books by Laura Ingalls Wilder
Children of the trail west by Holly Littlefield
We go together! by Todd Dunn
Going to town adapted from the Little house books by Laura Ingalls Wilder

Week Twenty-One

Your theme for this week will be *uncles, aunts, and other family members*. You will be focusing on the following topics with your child:

English – The letter U
Pre-Math – Circles and the number 0
Art – The color green

Lesson One Hundred and One – Monday

English: Recognition of the Letter U

Materials: Card stock
Umbrella pictures (see companion download)
Glue

Preparation: Cut a capital letter U out of card stock. Print several copies of the umbrella from the companion download.

Lesson: Let your child glue the umbrellas all over their capital U.

Pre-Math – Sorting

Materials: Old magazines or newspaper inserts
Construction paper (optional)
Glue stick (optional)

Preparation: Cut out pictures of baby items as well as items for older children (i.e., clothes, food, etc.)

Lesson:
1. Give your child the magazine pictures and have them sort the pictures into two piles – one of baby items and one of older child items.
2. You can have your child glue these items to different pieces of construction paper if you would like.

229

Art – Family Portrait

Materials: Paper plate
                    Yarn
                    Crayons or markers
                    Hole punch

Preparation: None

Lesson:
1. Have your child create a picture of their family on the inside of a plate. Encourage them to include their uncles, aunts, cousins and grandparents if possible.
2. Punch a hole at the top of the plate and thread a piece of yarn through it.
3. Hang the family portraits on the wall.

Gross Motor Skills – Walk the Zeros

Materials: Construction paper

Preparation: Cut large zeros from several pieces of large construction paper. You may want to laminate them to make them last longer.

Lesson:
1. Arrange the zeroes in any kind of pattern on the floor.
2. Have your child walk the pattern by placing their feet inside the zeroes.
3. Rearrange the zeros and have your child walk the pattern again.

Science – Baby Sensory

Materials: Baby oil
                    Baby shampoo
                    Baby lotion
                    Baby powder
                    Hard plastic doll (optional)

Preparation: None

Lesson:
1. Let your child use the different baby products on their doll.
2. A variation of this activity would be to dip cotton balls into each substance and play a smelling game with them instead. Or to let your child use these products on their own hands.

Literature -

Baby Babka : the gorgeous genius by Jane Breskin Zalben
A baby sister for Frances by Russell Hoban
Ain't nobody a stranger to me by Ann Grifalconi
Grandma, grandpa, and me by Mercer Mayer

Lesson One Hundred and Two – Tuesday

English – What I Like About My Family

Materials: Picture of your family
                   Construction paper
                   Glue stick
                   Crayons or pen

Preparation: None

Lesson:
1. Have your child glue the family photo to the construction paper.
2. Ask your child what they like about their family and write it down for them on the paper.

Pre-Math – Object Count

Materials: None

Preparation: None

Lesson:
1. Help your child to count various objects in the room and name a few objects for which there are none. For example, ask your child how many girls are in the room – then count the girls.
2. Then ask how many snakes are in the room. Your child will laugh and say "none."
3. Tell your child that another word for "none" is "zero." "There are zero snakes in our room."
4. Keep the game going as long as you wish, repeating zero as often as possible.
5. Another example would be "How many people with brown hair? How many with blonde hair? How many with purple hair?"
6. Let your child come up with their own outrageous questions.
7. And make a zero with your thumb and finger and/or help your child to trace out a zero in the air.

Fine Motor Skills – Grandparents Tea

Materials: Items for tea (i.e., tablecloth, teapot, teacups, etc.)

Preparation:
1. Help your child to make invitations for their grandparents to come to tea.
2. Ask around to borrow items to make it special.

Lesson:
1. The morning of the tea, encourage your child to help make cookies, help decorate, help set tables, etc.
2. When their grandparents arrive, ask them to tell your child stories about your family. Try to record these stories if it is at all possible.

History – Family Tree

Materials: Pictures of family members
               Poster board
               Markers
               Glue stick

Preparation:
1. Create a family tree with the correct number of branches on it for your family.
2. Try to do at least 3 generations – possibly 4 (your child, you and your husband, their grandparents, and their great-grandparents.)

Lesson: Help your child to glue the family photos onto the proper places in the family tree.

Literature -
Dad goes to school by Margaret McNamara
Mama, Papa, and Baby Joe by Niki Daly
What do parents do when you're not home by Jeanie Franz Ransom
Clifford's day with Dad by Norman Bridwell

Lesson One Hundred and Three – Wednesday

English – Family Collage

Materials: Old magazines or newspaper inserts
                    Construction paper
                    Glue stick
                    Crayons or markers

Preparation: None

Lesson:
1. Have your child cut out pictures of families from the magazines.
2. Let your children glue the families onto their paper.
3. Ask your child to give names to all of the people – write down their names for your child.

Pre-Math – Family Chart

Materials: Paper
                    Crayons
                    Glue stick

Preparation:
1. Create a graph which includes enough blank columns for each person in your family. Feel free to include extended family members on your graph as well.
2. Cut strips of paper out for each family member as well – tall strips for adults, small strips for children. You can use different colored paper to represent males and females, hair color, whatever you would prefer.

Lesson:
1. Ask your child to name each member of his family.
2. Write down the name of one family member beneath each column.
3. Hand out a strip of paper for each family member named by your child.
4. Let your child glue the strips of paper onto the graph.
5. Have your child count how many "people" are in his family.

Art – Hairy Hairdos

Materials: Glue
                      Various sizes of macaroni and spaghetti
                      2 Pieces of white paper

Preparation: None – unless you want to cook the spaghetti…

Lesson:
1. Give your child both pieces of paper.
2. Have your child draw a large circle on each piece. One piece will be for long things – the other piece for short things.
3. On the long sheet, have your child draw long eyes, a long nose and a long mouth. Then tell them to create a hairdo using long spaghetti.
4. On the short sheet, have your child draw short eyes, a short nose and a short mouth. Then tell them to create a hairdo using short pieces of macaroni.

Gross Motor Skills – Family Bowling

Materials: 5 2-liter soda bottles
                      Sand or water (optional)
                      Yarn
                      Permanent markers
                      Ball
                      Glue

Preparation:
1. Make the soda bottles look like people by using hair to make hair and permanent markers to draw faces.
2. You can fill the bottles 1/8 full with sand or water if you would like them to be a bit more stable. It will work just fine to leave them empty as well if you don't want to deal with the mess.

Lesson:
1. Set up the "family members" as you would bowling pins.
2. Have your child roll the ball toward the "people" and see how many he/she can knock over.

Science – Who Would Use This?

Materials: Different household items (slippers, tie, mixer, baby rattle, etc.)
                      Box to store items in

Preparation: None

Lesson: Have your child identify who in the family would use each item.

Literature -

Daddies : all about the work they do by Janet Frank
Daddies give you horsey rides by Abby Levine
The daddy book by Todd Parr
Daddy makes the best spaghetti by Anna Grossnickle Hines

Lesson One Hundred and Four – Thursday

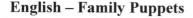

English – Family Puppets

Materials: Old magazines or newspaper inserts
             Glue
             Craft sticks
             Card stock
             Scissors

Preparation: None

Lesson:
1. Have your child cut out pictures of people who look like their family members from magazines.
2. Have your child glue these pictures onto the card stock.
3. When the glue is dry, let your child cut around the pictures.
4. Help your child to attach the pictures to a craft stick to make puppets.

Pre-Math – Bean Bag Toss

Materials: Large box
             Old magazines or newspaper inserts
             Glue
             Bean bags

Preparation:
1. Glue pictures of people onto the outside of the box.
2. Cut a large hole in the box.

Lesson:
1. Have your child try to toss their bean bags into the box.
2. Help your child to count how many times they throw the beanbag into the box.

Music – Dress Up and Dance

Materials: Old clothes (vests, funny hats, gloves, wigs, etc.)

Preparation: None

Lesson:
1. Let your child dress up to look like different family members.
2. Have your child walk and talk or sing and dance as if they were that family member.

Fine Motor Skills – Fold the Clothes

Materials: None

Preparation: Do a load of laundry so that there are fresh clothes to fold.

Lesson:
1. Show your child how to fold hand towels and washcloths.
2. Let them practice this with you whenever possible. It's a great help for you and it's wonderful for developing their fine motor skills.

Literature -
Before I was your mother by Kathryn Lasky
Every mom is special by Graham Jenks
Five minutes' peace by Jill Murphy
I love Mommy by Lizi Boyd

Lesson One Hundred and Five – Friday

English – I Love My Family Because…

Materials: Construction paper
               Crayons or markers

Preparation:
1. Use the construction paper to create a book – be sure there are enough pages for each member of your family.
2. Write the words "I love _____ because" on each page. Fill the in the blank with the names or titles of people in your family.

Lesson:
1. Show the book to your child.
2. Ask them what they love the most about each member of the family.
3. Write down their answers on each page – be sure to write what they say word-for-word.
4. After your child has given an answer for each family member, ask them to draw a picture of each person on their page.

Pre-Math – Numerical Order

Materials: 1-10 Flashcards

Preparation: None

Lesson:
1. Let your child try to put the flashcards in numerical order.
2. Mix them up and have them try it again. Let them continue until they can do it quickly without struggling.

Art – Picture Match

Materials: Baby pictures of family members
                    Current pictures of family members
                    Construction paper
                    Glue stick
                    Crayons or markers

Preparation: None

Lesson:
1. Scramble up the pictures and put them in front of your child.
2. Have your child see if they can match up the baby pictures with the correct current picture for each family member.
3. Let your child glue the pictures onto their paper.
4. You can help them to draw a tree and put leaves around each set of family member pictures if you would like. Otherwise, let your child use their imagination and draw whatever they would like.

Gross Motor Skills – Mother May I?

Materials: None

Preparation: None

Lesson:
1. Play the classic game (i.e., Mother may I take 3 baby steps forward?", etc.)
2. You can replace the word Mother with other family members if you would like.
3. Be sure to have your child do several different actions – scissor steps, skipping, jumping, etc.)

Science – Family Smells

Materials: Empty film canisters or other small containers
                    Familiar scents from around the house (coffee, perfume, spices, furniture polish, etc.)

Preparation: Fill the canisters with some familiar and/or favorite scents for your child.

Lesson: Let your child smell each canister and see if they can identify the scents.

Literature -
Kandoo Kangaroo hops into homeschool by Susan Ratner
If mom had three arms by Karen Kaufman Orloff
The aunt in our house by Angela Johnson
Auntee Edna by Ethel Smothers

Week Twenty-Two

Your theme for this week will be *Valentines*. You will be focusing on the following topics with your child:

English – The letter V
Pre-Math – Heart shapes and the number 0
Art – The color red

Lesson One Hundred and Six – Monday

English: Recognition of the Letter V

Materials: Card stock
                Red construction paper
                Glue stick

Preparation:
1. Cut a capital letter V out of card stock.
2. Cut several hearts out of the construction paper.

Lesson: Let your child glue "valentines" all over their capital V.

Pre-Math – Math Hearts

Materials: Box of conversation heart candies

Preparation: None

Lesson:
1. Let your child sort the hearts by color.
2. Let your child sort the hearts by message.
3. Help your child to count how many hearts are inside their box.
4. Let your child eat some of the hearts.

Art – Heart Rubbings

Materials: Sandpaper
                Paper
                Crayons

Preparation: Cut several hearts out of the sandpaper.

Lesson: Have your children place a piece of thin paper over the sandpaper hearts
                and rub with a crayon to form a design on their paper.

Fine Motor Skills – Valentine Postcard

Materials: Card stock
                Paper doily
                Small sponge (i.e., cosmetic sponge)
                Paint
                Crayons or markers

Preparation: Cut the card stock into postcard-sized pieces

Lesson:
1. Let your child place a paper doily over their postcard.
2. Have your child dip their sponge into the paint and then stamp the paint over the doily. NOTE: You should help them hold their doily in place so that it doesn't smear their design.
3. Have your child carefully remove the doily to reveal a Valentine's design.
4. After the paint dries, have your child dictate a message to their Valentine and you can write it down for them on their postcard.

Science – Grass Valentine

Materials: Sponge
                   Grass seeds (pick a fast sprouting variety like annual rye)
                   Water bottle
                   Plastic wrap
                   Plastic or terracotta saucer

Preparation: Cut the sponge into a heart shape and place it on a saucer.

Lesson:
1. Let your child moisten the sponge.
2. Have them sprinkle grass seeds all over the sponge.
3. Let them use the water bottle to spritz the seeds with water.
4. Help your child to cover the sponge with some plastic wrap to keep in the moisture.
5. Watch the seeds. Spritz them with water daily.
6. Once sprouts start to appear, you can remove the plastic wrap.
7. Let your child mow the grass with scissors as needed.
8. You should have a grassy heart within 2 weeks.

Literature –
The Most Precious Thing by Gill Lewis
Daddy's song by Leslea Newman
Did I tell you I love you today? by Deloris Jordan with Roslyn M. Jordan
Love, Ruby Valentine by Laurie Friedman

Lesson One Hundred and Seven – Tuesday

English – What is Love?

Materials: Construction paper
               Heart stickers
               Crayons or markers

Preparation:
1. Cut large hearts out of several pieces of construction paper.
2. On each page, write "Love is _____" or "I love _____ because _____."

Lesson:
1. Ask your child what love is – or what they love.
2. Write down whatever they say on their sheets.
3. Let your child decorate their hearts with the stickers and the crayons or markers.

Pre-Math – Fraction Hearts

Materials: Construction paper

Preparation:
1. Cut large hearts out of the construction paper.
2. Keep one heart whole.
3. Cut one heart in half.

Lesson:
1. Let your child see the whole heart. Ask them how many equal pieces the heart is divided into (1).
2. Put the half heart over the top of the whole heart. Ask your child how many equal pieces the heart is divided into, now (2).
3. Let your child play with the pieces and continue talking to them about halves and wholes.

Fine Motor Skills – Yummy Valentines

Materials: Graham crackers
               Pink or white frosting
               Plastic knife or cheese spreader
               Conversation heart candies or cinnamon candies

Preparation: None

Lesson: Let your child frost the graham crackers and then add the candies to the top as decorations. Let your child eat their yummy valentine.

Literature -
Homemade love by Bell Hooks
How do I love you? by P.K. Hallinan
How long? by Elizabeth Dale
How do I love you? by Leslie Kimmelman

Lesson One Hundred and Eight – Wednesday

English – Heart Creations

Materials: Pink, red, gray and white construction paper
                 Glue
                 Crayons or markers

Preparation: Cut out several hearts in all of the colors and in various sizes.

Lesson: Let your child make whatever they would like with the hearts. They can make snakes, flowers, rocket ships… let them go wherever their imaginations take them.

Pre-Math – Candy Box Numbers

Materials: Empty compartmentalized chocolates box
                 Red construction paper
                 Glue

Preparation:
1. Cut out squares the size of the compartments.
2. Write numbers on the squares and glue them into the compartments.
3. Cut out hearts and write corresponding numbers on them.

Lesson: Give your child the hearts and let them match the numbers on them to the numbers in the chocolate box.

Art – Heart Caterpillars

Materials: Pink and red construction paper
                 Glue stick
                 Heart stickers (optional)

Preparation: Cut several hearts out of the construction paper.

Lesson:
1. Let your child create a caterpillar with the hearts. Let them put the larger hearts together for the body.
2. They can decorate the body with smaller hearts or stickers.
3. Let your child glue on smaller hearts for eyes and to create the antennae.

Fine Motor Skills – Valentines Mailboxes

Materials: White lunch bag
               Small sponge (i.e., cosmetic sponge)
               Paint
               Hole punch
               Red ribbon

Preparation: Cut a heart shape out of the sponge.

Lesson:
1. Let your child sponge paint hearts all over their bag.
2. Once the paint is dry, fold the edges of the bag over twice and help your child to punch holes around the edges about one every inch.
3. Let your child weave a red ribbon through the holes and then help them to tie a bow.
4. Let them use this bag to collect any valentines that they might receive (if your child doesn't normally get valentine's cards, encourage grandparents or siblings to give out cards this year.)

Valentine's Sun Catchers

Materials: Wax paper
               Crayon shavings
               Towel
               Iron
               Hole punch
               Yarn

Preparation: Cut 2 pieces of wax paper into the shape of a heart.

Lesson:
1. Have your child sprinkle the crayon shavings onto one of the heart pieces and then cover them with the other heart shape.
2. Make sure the hearts are lined up with each other and place a towel over the hearts.
3. Hold a warm iron on the towel (with the steam turned off) for about 25 seconds.
4. Remove the towel and punch a hole in the top of the heart.
5. Tie a piece of yarn through the hold so that you can hang it up in a window.
6. Talk with your child about the changes in the colors.

Literature -
I love you always and forever by Jonathan Emmett
I love you because you're you by Liza Baker
If kisses were colors by Janet Lawler
Joy by Joyce Carol Thomas

Lesson One Hundred and Nine – Thursday

English – Find the Puzzle Piece

Materials: Red and pink card stock

Preparation: Cut out 7 differently-sized hearts from red and pink card stock. Cut each heart into a different two-pieced puzzle.

Lesson:
1. Place one half of each heart on one side of the table and the other half on the other side of the table. Make sure they are mixed up.
2. Have your child pick a heart half from the left side and have them fit it together with the corresponding heart from the right side – to form a complete heart.

Pre-Math – Graph Hearts

Materials: Box of conversation heart candies
                    Paper
                    Crayons or markers

Preparation: None

Lesson:
1. Let your child sort the hearts by color. Help your child to graph the results.
2. Let your child sort the hearts by message. Help your child to graph the results.
3. Let your child eat some of the hearts.

Music – Valentine's Shaker

Materials: Popped popcorn
                    2 Paper plates
                    Stapler
                    Red construction paper
                    Glue stick

Preparation: Draw hearts on the red construction paper.

Lesson:
1. Help your child to cut the hearts out of the red paper.
2. Let your child glue them all over the outsides of their plates.
3. Have your child put the popcorn inside the plates and staple them together.
4. Sing a few songs and let your child keep time with their Valentine's shaker.

Fine Motor Skills – Guess How Much I Love You Card

Materials: Card stock
                Red construction paper
                Butcher or parchment paper
                Glue stick
                Measuring tape

Preparation:
1. Cut out two hearts for your child.
2. Fold a piece of cardstock in half to make a card.
3. On the first heart, write "Guess how much I love you?"
4. On the second heart, write "This much!"

Lesson:
1. Measure the distance between the fingertips of one hand to the fingertips of the other hand with your child's arms stretched out wide.
2. Cut out this distance from the butcher or parchment paper.
3. Help your child to fold the paper like an accordion.
4. Help your child to attach the hearts to each end of their butcher paper.
5. Let them give the card to the person of their choice. This is a great idea for grandparents! ☺

Science – Sand Art Cookies

Materials: ½ cup white sugar
                 ½ cup rolled oats
                 ½ cup candy-coated chocolate pieces
                 ½ cup packed brown sugar
                 1 ¼ cup all-purpose flour
                 ½ tsp baking powder
                 ½ tsp salt
                 ½ cup Rice Krispies
                 ½ cup semisweet chocolate chips

Preparation: None

Lesson:
1. In a 1 quart or 1 liter jar, layer the ingredients in the order given.
2. Lightly pack down the jar after each addition.
3. Attach a card with the following instructions:

   Preheat oven to 350 degrees F (175 degrees C). Grease a cookie sheet. Empty the entire contents of the jar into a medium bowl. Add 1 large egg and 1/2 cup of margarine melted; mix well. Form dough into 1 inch balls and bake for 10 to 12 minutes in the preheated oven. Makes about 2 dozen cookies.

4. Encourage your child to decorate the jar and give it as a gift for Valentine's Day (possibly to Sunday School teachers, pastors, or grandparents.)

Literature –
Guess How Much I Love You by Sam Bratney
Milly, Molly and I love you by Gill Pittar
The most important gift of all by David Conway
No matter what by Debi Gliori

Lesson One Hundred and Ten – Friday

English – Mini Color Album

Materials: Old magazines or newspaper inserts
Small photo album (like the kind you get from
Walmart when you get your pictures developed)
Paper
Pen or marker
Scissors

Preparation: None

Lesson:
1. Let your child cut out pictures of "red items" from the magazines and place them in their photo album.
2. Make labels for each item and stick them underneath or next to the pictures.
3. Young children can't read these words, yet, but this activity will expose them to language.

Pre-Math – Hearts Guess

Materials: Candy conversation hearts

Preparation: None

Lesson:
1. Have your child guess how many hearts are in their box.
2. Help your child to count their hearts.
3. Let your child eat some of their hearts.

Art – Heart Pins

Materials: Clay
                    Heart cookie cutter
                    Safety pin
                    Red paint
                    Glitter

Preparation: None

Lesson:
1. Help your child to cut out a heart shape using the cookie cutter.
2. Push a pin into the back of the heart.
3. Bake the clay and let it cool.
4. Let your child decorate their heart with paint and glitter.

Fine Motor Skills – Beaded Heart

Materials: Pipe cleaner
                    Beads

Preparation: None

Lesson:
1. Let your child string beads onto the pipe cleaner until it is as full as desired.
2. Help your child to bend their pipe cleaner into a V shape.
3. Finish by helping them to shape their V into a heart.
4. Twist the ends of the pipe cleaner together so the beads will stay on.

Science – Valentine's Field Trip

Materials: Paper
                    Envelope
                    Stamp
                    Various art supplies

Preparation: None

Lesson:
1. Help your child to make a Valentine for each member of your family.
2. Help your child to put the Valentine into the envelope, address the envelope and put on the stamp.
3. Take a trip to the post office and let your child put the envelope into the mailbox.
4. If possible, arrange a guided visit to the post office so that your child can see what goes on behind the scenes.

Literature -
<u>Oh my baby, little one</u> by Kathi Appelt
<u>The teddy bear</u> by David McPhail
<u>That's love</u> by Sam Williams
<u>Corduroy</u> by Don Freeman

Week Twenty-Three

Your theme for this week will be *weather*. You will be focusing on the following topics with your child:

English – The letter W
Pre-Math – Circles and the numbers 1-5
Art – The color yellow

Lesson One Hundred and Eleven - Monday

English: Recognition of the Letter W

Materials: Card stock
                Wood shavings
                Glue

Preparation: Cut a capital letter W out of card stock.

Lesson: Let your child cover their capital W with wood shavings.

Pre-Math – Balls of Snow

Materials: White construction paper
                Yellow construction paper

Preparation: Cut out white circles in various sizes.

Lesson: Instruct your child to create a snowman using six snowballs – this will require them to count the correct number of circles.

Art – Snow Painting

Materials: Whipped cream
                Blue construction paper

Preparation: None

Lesson: Let your child finger-paint a snow picture onto their paper.

Gross Motor Skills – Windy Weather Catch

Materials: Light objects (scarf, Kleenex, etc.)
Hair dryer

Preparation: None

Lesson: Blow the objects into the air with the hair dryer and have your child try to catch them.

Science – The Wind

Materials: None

Preparation: None

Lesson:
1. Talk to your child about the wind. Tell them how the wind blows the clouds around in the sky.
2. Ask them if they have ever had anything blow away.
3. On a really windy day, take your child outside and show them the effect the wind has on some ordinary items (i.e., paper plate, sheet, leaves, etc.)

Literature -
The Wind Blew by Pat Hutchins
The Day of the Wind, Rain and Snow by Robert Pierce
When Will it Snow? by Bruce Hiscock
The Snowy Day by Ezra Jack Keats

Lesson One Hundred and Twelve – Tuesday

English – Making Maple Taffy

Materials: Clean snow or shaved ice
                Pure maple syrup
                Small pans
                Candy thermometer

Preparation: None

Lesson:
1. Boil the maple syrup.
2. Let your child gather some clean snow and bring it inside.
3. Let your child draw small paths in the snow with their fingers – possibly the first letter in their name.
4. Once the maple syrup gets to the soft ball stage it is ready to use. Be sure to watch the syrup CAREFULLY because it will boil over easily and will be VERY HARD to clean off of your stove. ☺
5. Help your child to fill the paths with the maple syrup.
6. The syrup should cool very quickly. Peel it off of the snow with your fingers and enjoy.

Pre-Math – Numerical Order

Materials: 1-10 Flashcards

Preparation: None

Lesson:
1. Let your child try to put the flashcards in numerical order.
2. Mix them up and have them try it again. Let them continue until they can do it quickly without struggling.

Fine Motor Skills – Wind and Clouds

Materials: Straws
                Cotton balls or pompoms

Preparation: None

Lesson:
1. Discuss how the wind moves the clouds.
2. Have a cloud race with your child by blowing into the straws to move the cotton balls or pompoms.

Science – Bag of Rain

Materials: Piece of sod (grass with soil attached)
                      Ziploc bag
                      Straw
                      Water
                      Masking tape

Preparation: None

Lesson:
1. Help your child to dig up a small piece of sod and put it into the Ziploc bag.
2. Pour a couple of spoonfuls of water over the grass.
3. Stick the straw into the bag.
4. Seal the rest of the bag.
5. Using the straw, fill the bag with air. Then remove the straw and seal the bag the rest of the way.
6. Tape the bag to a window that receives a lot of sun.
7. After awhile, you will see drops of water forming at the top of the bag.
8. Once a drop gets big enough, it will roll down the sides of the bag.
9. Let your child watch their bag of rain.

Literature -
It's Raining, It's Pouring by Kin Eagle
Katy and the Big Snow by Virginia Lee Burton
Gilberto and the Wind by Marie Hall Ets
Mushroom in the Rain by Mirra Ginsburg

Lesson One Hundred and Thirteen – Wednesday

English – Wiggly Worms

Materials: Brads
Construction paper
Scissors
Hole punch

Preparation: None

Lesson:
1. Let your child create their own worms by cutting segments from the paper and connecting the segments with the brads.
2. Be sure to let your child do the hole punching and inserting of the brads – this is excellent for developing fine motor skills as well as hand-eye coordination.

Pre-Math – Ice Colors

Materials: 2 or 3 ice cubes
Ziploc bag
Food coloring

Preparation: None

Lesson:
1. Put the ice cubes and a few drops of food coloring into the bag.
2. Be sure the bag is sealed well.
3. Let your child partially melt the ice cubes by handling the bag.
4. Add a different color of food coloring to the bag and reseal it.
5. Let your child handle the bag again and see what happens as the two colors mix together.

Art – Cloud Pieces

Materials: White paper
              Blue construction paper
              Cotton balls
              Glue
              Scissors

Preparation: None

Lesson:
1. Let your child cut the white paper to look like a cloud.
2. Then let your child glue cotton balls to their cloud.
3. Let your child glue their clouds onto the construction paper to make a sky scene.

Gross Motor Skills – Hide the Sun

Materials: Flashlight

Preparation: None

Lesson:
1. Play flashlight tag with your child – only have the flashlight be the sun.
2. If the "sunlight" hits you then you are "it."

Science – Sun's Energy

Materials: 4 Ziploc bags
              White paper
              Orange paper
              Black paper
              Aluminum foil

Preparation: None

Lesson:
1. Fill the four Ziploc bags with water.
2. Talk to your child about how different colors attract sunlight. Then ask your child which color would make their bag the hottest if they leave them in the sun.
3. Put the bags in a sunny window – one covered with white paper, one with orange, one with black and one with the aluminum foil.
4. Leave the bags in the window for a couple of hours and see which one gets the hottest.
5. (Optional) You may want to help your child graph the results.

Literature -
<u>Clouds Kazuo</u> by Nizaka
<u>Cloud Dance</u> by Thomas Locker
<u>Thunder Cake</u> by Patricia Polacco
<u>Carl's nose</u> by Karen Lee Schmidt

Lesson One Hundred and Fourteen – Thursday

English – Water Cycle

Materials: This is the rain by Lola M. Schaefer

Preparation: None

Lesson:
1. Read This is the rain by Lola M. Schaefer.
2. Discuss the water cycle with your child.

Pre-Math – Measuring Rainfall (or snowfall depending on where you live)

Materials: Rain gauge (or plastic glass)
              Paper

Preparation: Make a chart to measure the rainfall.

Lesson:
1. On a rainy day, set out the rain gauge or a container to measure the rainfall.
2. At the end of the day, measure the rainfall.
3. Continue to measure the rain each day and record it for at least a week.
4. Ask your child to predict how much rain will be collected.

Music – Weather Music

Materials: Eye of the Storm [Sound Recording] – thunderstorm CD

Preparation: None

Lesson: Play the weather CD while your child works on their other schoolwork.

Fine Motor Skills – Baster Play

Materials: Turkey baster
                  2 Large bowls

Preparation: None

Lesson:
1. Fill one of the bowls full of water.
2. Show your child how to suck water into the baster and transfer it from one bowl to another.
3. Let your child try to transfer as much water as possible from one bowl to the other. Be sure to do this on a floor which can be mopped afterwards because it's probably going to get wet.

Science – Weather Dial

Materials: Paper plate
                  Paper
                  Brad
                  Crayons

Preparation:
1. Draw an arrow on the paper.
2. Divide the plate into four different sections.

Lesson:
1. Have your child draw a different weather day in each section (sunny day, rainy day, cloudy day, and snowy day)
2. Help your child to cut out their arrow.
3. Have your child attach the arrow to their plate with the brad.
4. On each day, have your child look out the window and move the arrow on the weather dial to whichever kind of day you are having.

Literature -
<u>Hello, sun!</u> by Dayle Ann Dodds
<u>If frogs made the</u> weather by Marion Dane Bauer
<u>Sunny Sunday drive</u> by Janine Scott
<u>Hello sun!</u> by Hans Wilhelm

Lesson One Hundred and Fifteen – Friday

English – Types of Clouds

Materials: Construction paper
Pictures of clouds (see companion download)
Crayons or markers

Preparation: Print the clouds from the companion download.

Lesson:
1. Discuss the different types of clouds with your child – show them pictures from the companion download.
2. Let your child draw a picture or make a book of clouds.

Pre-Math – Graph the Weather

Materials: Paper
Crayons

Preparation: Create a graph with sunny day, rainy day, cloudy day, and snowy day categories.

Lesson: Help your child to graph the weather for the next several weeks.

Art – Painting

Materials: Watercolor paints
Paper
Newspaper

Preparation: Cover the work surface with newspapers.

Lesson: Let your child paint a watercolor picture.

Gross Motor Skills – Winter Dress Up

Materials: Your child's winter clothing

Preparation: None

Lesson: Let your child practice putting on their winter gear – including zipping, buttoning, snapping, tying, etc.

Science – Wind Stick

Materials: Empty paper towel roll
                  Tissue paper or crepe paper
                  Paint
                  Stapler

Preparation: Cut some tissue paper into strips – or just use crepe paper.

Lesson:
1. Have your child paint their paper towel roll.
2. Once the paint dries, help your child to staple their tissue paper or crepe paper strips to the end of the roll.
3. On a windy day, let your child take their stick outside and watch the strips blow in the wind.

Literature -
Froggy gets dressed by Jonathan London
Little Bear by Else Holmelund Minarik
Winter white by Christianne C. Jones
The winter visitors by Karel Hayes

Week Twenty-Four

Your theme for this week will be *x-rays and our amazing bodies*. You will be focusing on the following topics with your child:

English – The letter X
Pre-Math – Squares and the numbers 1-5
Art – The color blue

Lesson One Hundred and Sixteen – Monday

English: Recognition of the Letter X

Materials: Card stock
                White paper
                Blue paint
                Newspaper
                Bone shape (see companion download)
                Paint smock or an old shirt
                Glue stick

Preparation: Cut a capital letter X out of card stock. Cut out bone shapes from the white paper.

Lesson:
1. Have your child put on their paint smock or an old shirt to protect their clothing. Have them roll up the sleeves to minimize the mess.
2. Spread the newspapers out to protect your work surface and let your child paint their X.
3. After your child's X is dry, let them glue the bones all over their letter X.

Pre-Math – Collecting By Likeness

Materials: Paper lunch bag
              Various shapes and colors of blocks

Preparation: None

Lesson:
    1. Give your child the paper bag and have him or her fill it with various blocks by likeness (i.e., "all of the triangle blocks", "all of the blue blocks", etc.
    2. As they put each item in the bag, have them explain to you why it belongs in the bag (what it has in common with the other items.)

Art – X-Ray

Materials: Black paper
              Chalk
              Picture of x-rays (see companion download)

Preparation: Print the pictures of x-rays from the companion download.

Lesson:
    1. Show your child the pictures of the x-rays.
    2. Talk to them about why they might need to have an x-ray taken someday.
    3. Have your child draw a simple x-ray on their paper with the chalk.

Gross Motor Skills – Sticky Feet

Materials: Contact paper
              Masking tape

Preparation:
    1. Cut a piece of contact paper at least 2 feet long.
    2. Removing the backing and tape the paper to the floor sticky-side up.

Lesson: Have your child take off their socks and let them run, jump, dance or just stand on the contact paper.

Science – Skeleton and X-Rays

Materials: A skeleton
                 Old x-rays (ask a doctor for old ones)

Preparation: None

Lesson:
    1. Let your child touch, see and move the different bones on the skeleton.
    2. Let them examine the x-rays.
    3. Talk to them about what they observe.

Literature -
Jessica's x-ray by Pat Zonta
At the doctor by Chris Forsey
Our skeleton by Susan Thames
Breathing by Angela Royston

Lesson One Hundred and Seventeen – Tuesday

English – Teeth?

Materials: White board and markers

Preparation: None

Lesson:
1. Talk to your child about teeth – why they have them, etc.
2. Discuss animals that have teeth and those that do not.
3. Help your child to make a list. Be sure to let your child come up with as many animals on their own as they can.

Pre-Math – Paper Plate Mouth

Materials: Small paper plate
              Mini marshmallows
              Glue

Preparation: None

Lesson:
1. Let your child glue the marshmallows around the edge of their plate (to be teeth.)
2. When the glue has dried, fold the plate in half.
3. Have your child count the marshmallows.

Gross Motor Skills – Exercise

Materials: None

Preparation: None

Lesson: You and your child take turns prescribing physical activities to each other. "Doctor Zack says jump up and down 3 times", etc.

Science – Listen to My Heart

Materials: Empty toilet paper tube

Preparation: None

Lesson: Have your child place the tube on your chest and let them listen to your heart.

Literature -
Cousin Ruth's tooth by Amy MacDonald
Brush well : a look at dental care by Katie Bagley
The story of the heart by Sandra Magsamen with Linell Smith
Hear your heart by Paul Showers

Lesson One Hundred and Eighteen – Wednesday

English – From Head to Toe

Materials: From Head to Toe by Eric Carle

Preparation: None

Lesson:
1. Read the book to your child.
2. While you're reading the book, act it out with your children (i.e., if it says, "I am a crocodile and I can wriggle my hips" then show them how to do the action.
3. Then say, "Can you do it?"
4. Have your child say "I can do it!" and then have them give it a try.

Pre-Math – Footprint Fun

Materials: None

Preparation: None

Lesson:
1. On a day that the snow has just fallen, ask your child to describe the snow on the ground. (If you live in a warmer climate, do this after some rain instead.)
2. Have your child put on their snow gear and walk across the snow (or through a water puddle.)
3. Have them turn around and look at their footprints.
4. Have your child follow their footprints back to the house.
5. Ask your child to count the footprints as they take steps.

Art – Head Reflector Art

Materials: Construction paper
              Stapler or tape
              Card stock
              Aluminum foil
              Permanent marker

Preparation: Cut out a circle from the card stock.

Lesson:
1. Help your child to cut out two strips of construction paper that will fit around their head when connected.
2. Connect the strips with tape or staples.
3. Give your child the circle and a piece of aluminum foil.
4. Have your child wrap the aluminum foil around the circle.
5. Staple the circle to the construction paper.
6. Write Doctor Zack or Doctor Sally or whoever they'd like to be on the headband.
7. Let your child pretend to be a doctor and you can pretend to be the patient.

Gross Motor Skills – Body Part Musical Squares

Materials: Paper
              Markers
              Music CD

Preparation: Draw different body parts on each piece of paper. Place the papers randomly on the floor.

Lesson:
1. Have your child stand on one of the squares.
2. Start playing the music and have your child move around the room in whatever way you tell them (i.e., crawl, walk backwards, hop, etc.)
3. When the music stops your child must go to the square closest to them and touch whatever body part is drawn on that square.

Science – Jello X-ray

Materials: Package of Jello
                  Fruit

Preparation: Make the Jello with fruit in it.

Lesson:
1. Explain to your child that their snack is like an x-ray. You can see the fruit even though it is inside the Jello. With an x-ray, you can see your bones even though they are inside of your body.
2. Let your child enjoy eating their x-ray snack.

Literature -
<u>Air is all around you</u> by Franklyn M. Branley
<u>I can tell by touching</u> by Carolyn Otto
<u>My five senses</u> by Aliki
<u>On the move</u> by Deborah Heiligman

Lesson One Hundred and Nineteen – Thursday

English – Feet Butterflies

Materials: Paint
                Construction paper
                Crayons or markers

Preparation: None

Lesson:
1. Have your child take off their socks and sit in a chair.
2. Paint the bottoms of their feet.
3. Bring the paper over to where your child is sitting and have them step onto the paper with their feet and heels together.
4. Wash off your child's feet.
5. Once their paper is dry, help your child to add antennae with markers or crayons.
6. Have your child dictate a story about their butterfly and write it on their paper for them.

Pre-Math – Candy Land

Materials: Candy Land game

Preparation: None

Lesson:
1. Play Candy Land with your child.
2. Be sure to let your child identify the colors on the cards and the game board as often as they possibly can.
3. If your child seems hesitant to identify the color blue, encourage them that they know this color as they have been studying it all week.

Music – Name Song

Materials: None

Preparation: None

Lesson: Sing a song about your child's name to the tune of Bingo:

There is a child that I know best
And Sammy is his name-o.
S-A-M-M-Y, S-A-M-M-Y, S-A-M-M-Y,
And Sammy is his name-o.

Fine Motor Skills – How to Brush your Teeth

Materials: Toothbrush
               Dental disclosing tablets
               Floss
               Toothpaste

Preparation: None

Lesson:
1. Let your child brush their teeth as they normally would.
2. Have your child chew a dental disclosing tablet which will turn the plaque a dark red.
3. Help show your child how to properly brush and floss their teeth and show them how that gets rid of the red.
4. You can do this with your child for several days until they get into the habit of brushing well.

Science – Our Daily Body Parts

Materials: None

Preparation: None

Lesson:
1. Go over the various body parts with your child.
2. Start with their head and work your way down.
3. To help them remember and to make it fun, come up with cute sayings such as "our eyes blink" or "our nose beeps" or "our toes wiggle" etc.
4. Talk to your child about the five different senses that their body parts give them (sight, smell, taste, touch, and hearing).

Literature -
Sleep is for everyone by Paul Showers
Sounds all around by Wendy Pfeffer
Germs make me sick! by Melvin Berger
What happens to a hamburger? by Paul Showers

Lesson One Hundred and Twenty – Friday

English – I Like...

Materials: Paper
                 Crayons or markers

Preparation: None

Lesson:
1. Have your child make a book which includes a page for each person they know.
2. Write the words "I Like _____ because _____" and have your child tell you what they like best about each person. Write down their exact words on each page.
3. Have your child draw a picture illustrating each page.

Pre-Math – Foot Measurement

Materials: Paper
                 Marker

Preparation: None

Lesson:
1. Trace your child's foot.
2. Help your child to cut out their footprint.
3. Laminate the footprint.
4. Ask your child use their footprint to find items which are shorter than their foot.
5. Have them find items which are longer than their foot.

Art – Band Aid Art

Materials: Band aids
                 Paper

Preparation: None

Lesson: Let your child stick the band aids on their paper to make a picture.

Gross Motor Skills – Sheet Day

Materials: Sheets
     Chairs
     Rubber bands and/or ponytail holders

Preparation: None

Lesson: Let your child create houses, tents, forts, or anything else they can dream
     up using. Use rubber bands or ponytail holders to attach the sheets to the
     chairs, etc.

Science – Large Teeth

Materials: 2-Liter bottles
     White paint
     Toothbrush

Preparation: Cut the bottom off of the 2-liter bottles. Paint the bottoms white.

Lesson: Use the "teeth" to show your children how to properly brush their teeth.

Literature -
Eyes by Cynthia Klingel & Robert B. Noyed
Why I sneeze, shiver, hiccup, and yawn by Mel Berger
Ears by Cynthia Klingel & Robert B. Noyed
Feet by Cynthia Klingel & Robert B. Noyed

Week Twenty-Five

Your theme for this week will be *yahoo, its spring*. You will be focusing on the following topics with your child:

English – The letter Y
Pre-Math – Oval and the number 6-10
Art – The color brown

Lesson One Hundred and Twenty-One – Monday

English: Recognition of the Letter Y

Materials: Card stock
Apple
Yellow paint
Newspaper
Paint smock or an old shirt

Preparation: Cut a capital letter Y out of card stock.

Lesson:
1. Have your child put on their paint smock or an old shirt to protect their clothing. Have them roll up the sleeves to minimize the mess.
2. Spread the newspapers out to protect your work surface.
3. Let your child paint their letter Y. Let their project dry.

Pre-Math – Planting Flowers

Materials: Construction paper or wallpaper scraps
Craft sticks
Flower pot
Sand
Number flashcards 1-10

Preparation:
1. Fill the flower pot with sand.
2. Cut out 12 flower shapes out of the construction paper or wallpaper scraps.
3. Glue the flowers to the craft sticks.

Lesson: Have your child draw a number flashcard and then plant the correct number of flowers in the flower pot.

Art – Paper Plate Daisy

Materials: Paper plate
                  Yellow construction paper
                  Glue
                  Paint or markers

Preparation: Cut flower petals out of the construction paper.

Lesson:
1. Let your child paint their entire plate.
2. Once the paint dries, let your child glue the flower petals around the outside of their plate.

Gross Motor Skills – Caterpillar Role Play

Materials: Blanket

Preparation: None

Lesson:
1. Have your children act out the stages of a butterfly.
2. Caterpillar = have your child crawl on the ground pretending to eat everything.
3. Cocoon = have your child roll up into a blanket and then slowly uncoil.
4. Butterfly – have them flap their arms and fly/run around the room.

Science – Bug Watch

Materials: Magnifying glass (optional)
                  A few crumbs of food, such as bread (optional)

Preparation: None

Lesson:
1. Go outside with your child and look for bugs.
2. Watch them do their work.
3. (optional) Put down a food crumb and see if any ants will pick it up.

Literature -
Are you spring? by Caroline Pitcher
Cold little duck, duck, duck by Lisa Westberg Peters
Goose moon by Carolyn Arden
Henry and Mudge in puddle trouble by Cynthia Rylant

Lesson One Hundred and Twenty-Two – Tuesday

English – Busy Bugs Headbands

Materials: Construction paper
                Stapler or tape
                Two pipe cleaners
                Permanent marker

Preparation: None

Lesson:
1. Help your child to cut out two strips of construction paper that will fit around their head when connected.
2. Connect the strips with tape or staples.
3. Give your child two pipe cleaners and let them shape them however they would like.
4. Help your child to staple the pipe cleaners to their headband.
5. Write "Busy Bee Timmy" or "Beautiful Butterfly Ben" or whoever they'd like to be on the headband.

Pre-Math – Butterfly Match

Materials: Construction paper
                Butterfly shape (see companion download)

Preparation: Using the butterfly shape from the companion download, create several different colored butterflies and cut them in half.

Lesson: Give your child the butterfly halves and let them put them back together correctly.

Art – Insect Collage

Materials: Contact paper
                Various colors of tissue paper
                Insect shapes (see companion download)

Preparation: Using the outlines in the companion download, cut the contact paper out into the shape of several insects.

Lesson:
1. Take the back off of the contact paper and place it sticky-side up in front of your child.
2. Let your child rip off small pieces of tissue paper and stick them onto the contact paper.
3. These will make great insect collages. Hang them up in the window and watch the light shine through them.

Fine Motor Skills – Bee Strips

Materials: Yellow construction paper
                Black construction paper
                Bee outline (see companion download)
                Scissors
                Glue stick
                Crayons or markers

Preparation: Using the outline from the companion download, cut out a bee shape from the yellow construction paper.

Lesson:
1. Let your child cut strips out of the black construction paper.
2. Help your child to glue the black stripes onto their bee.
3. Let your child finish decorating their bee with crayons or markers.

Science – Raise A Butterfly

Materials: Caterpillar
               Leaves
               Wide mouth jar
               Netting or a piece of nylon

Preparation: None

Lesson:
1. Go outside on a caterpillar hunt. You can find caterpillars on many plants in the spring and early summer.
2. Put the caterpillar and a few fresh leaves into the jar.
3. Cover the jar mouth with netting or a piece of nylon.
4. Change the leaves every day and provide dry paper towels to help prevent mold.
5. You can put in pencil-sized twigs for the caterpillar to attach its chrysalis or cocoon.
6. The insect will hatch in 10-14 days if it doesn't overwinter.
7. Release your butterfly or moth outside.

Literature –
The Very Hungry Caterpillar by Eric Carle
The Itsy Bitsy Spider by Iza Trapani
The Very Busy Spider by Eric Carle
Will Spring be Early? Or Will Spring be Late? by Crockett Johnson

Lesson One Hundred and Twenty-Three - Wednesday

English – The Ants Go Marching Book

Materials: Construction paper
              Colored rice or dried beans
              Glue
              Crayons or markers

Preparation: None

Lesson:
1. Help your child make a book so that each verse has its own page. Let them glue the correct amount of rice or beans to each page.
2. Let your child decorate their pages with the crayons or markers.

Pre-Math – Caterpillar Jar

Materials: Empty jar
              Gummy worms

Preparation: Put the gummy worms into the jar.

Lesson:
1. Have your child guess how many worms are in the jar.
2. Help your child to count the worms.
3. Let them eat their gummy worms.

Art – Rock Bug

Materials: Rock
              Paint or markers
              Pipe cleaners
              Tacky glue
              Google eyes

Preparation: None

Lesson:
1. Help your child to go outside and pick their own rock.
2. Wash the rock and let it dry.
3. Give your child the various art materials and let them design their own bug.

Music – Baby Bumblebee

Materials: None

Preparation: None

Lesson: Sing the song with your child:

Baby Bumble Bee Song
I'm bringing home a baby bumblebee,
Won't my mommy be so proud of me,
(Cup hands together as if holding bee)
I'm bringing home a baby bumblebee,
Ouch! It stung me!
(Shake hands as if just stung)

I'm squishing up the baby bumblebee,
Won't my mommy be so proud of me,
('Squish' bee between palms of hands)
I'm squishing up a baby bumblebee,
Ooh! It's yucky!
(Open up hands to look at 'mess')

I'm wiping off the baby bumblebee,
Won't my mommy be so proud of me,
(Wipe hands off on shirt)
I'm wiping off the baby bumblebee,
Now my mommy won't be mad at me!
(Hold hands up to show they are clean)

Science – Flowers Food

Materials: White carnation
               Food coloring
               Glass or vase of water

Preparation: None

Lesson:
1. Use the food coloring to color the water in the glass or vase. (Use a darker color)
2. Put the carnation into the glass and observe.
3. The flower's color will change as it takes in the water. This will take several days to get the full effect so keep looking.

Literature -
<u>Gregory's Shadow</u> by Don Freeman
<u>Wake me in Spring</u> by James Preller
<u>Make Way for Ducklings</u> by Robert McCloskey
<u>Signs of spring</u> by Justine Korman Fontes

Lesson One Hundred and Twenty-Four - Thursday

English – The Great Corn and Bean Race

Materials: 2 Clear plastic cups
Potting soil
Measuring tape or ruler
Paper
Corn seeds
Bean seeds

Preparation: Create a chart with 2 columns, one labeled *corn* and the other labeled *beans*.

Lesson:
1. Help your child to plant bean seeds in one cup and corn seeds in the other.
2. Ask your child to predict which seeds will grow faster.
3. Watch the plants grow and measure them with the measuring tape or ruler.
4. Help your child to record their finding on the chart.

Pre-Math – The Ants Go Marching

Materials: None

Preparation: None

Lesson: Sing and dance to "The Ants Go Marching" song.

The ants go marching one by one, hurrah, hurrah
The ants go marching one by one, hurrah, hurrah
The ants go marching one by one,
The little one stops to suck his thumb
And they all go marching down to the ground
To get out of the rain, BOOM! BOOM! BOOM!

The ants go marching two by two, hurrah, hurrah
The ants go marching two by two, hurrah, hurrah
The ants go marching two by two,
The little one stops to tie his shoe
And they all go marching down to the ground
To get out of the rain, BOOM! BOOM! BOOM!

The ants go marching three by three, hurrah, hurrah
The ants go marching three by three, hurrah, hurrah
The ants go marching three by three,
The little one stops to climb a tree
And they all go marching down to the ground
To get out of the rain, BOOM! BOOM! BOOM!

The ants go marching four by four, hurrah, hurrah
The ants go marching four by four, hurrah, hurrah
The ants go marching four by four,
The little one stops to shut the door
And they all go marching down to the ground
To get out of the rain, BOOM! BOOM! BOOM!

The ants go marching five by five, hurrah, hurrah
The ants go marching five by five, hurrah, hurrah
The ants go marching five by five,
The little one stops to take a dive
And they all go marching down to the ground
To get out of the rain, BOOM! BOOM! BOOM!

The ants go marching six by six, hurrah, hurrah
The ants go marching six by six, hurrah, hurrah
The ants go marching six by six,
The little one stops to pick up sticks
And they all go marching down to the ground
To get out of the rain, BOOM! BOOM! BOOM!

The ants go marching seven by seven, hurrah, hurrah
The ants go marching seven by seven, hurrah, hurrah
The ants go marching seven by seven,
The little one stops to pray to heaven
And they all go marching down to the ground
To get out of the rain, BOOM! BOOM! BOOM!

The ants go marching eight by eight, hurrah, hurrah
The ants go marching eight by eight, hurrah, hurrah
The ants go marching eight by eight,
The little one stops to shut the gate
And they all go marching down to the ground
To get out of the rain, BOOM! BOOM! BOOM!

The ants go marching nine by nine, hurrah, hurrah
The ants go marching nine by nine, hurrah, hurrah
The ants go marching nine by nine,
The little one stops to check the time
And they all go marching down to the ground
To get out of the rain, BOOM! BOOM! BOOM!

The ants go marching ten by ten, hurrah, hurrah
The ants go marching ten by ten, hurrah, hurrah
The ants go marching ten by ten,
The little one stops to say "THE END"
And they all go marching down to the ground
To get out of the rain, BOOM! BOOM! BOOM!

Art – Paper Gardens

Materials: Easter grass
Pipe cleaners
Construction paper
Muffin liners
Crayons or markers
Glue

Preparation: None

Lesson:
1. Have your children glue the Easter grass onto their paper.
2. Let them design their own gardens using the rest of the art supplies.

Science – Solar Ovens

Materials: Aluminum foil
Shoe box
Kabob skewers
Plastic wrap
Marshmallows

Preparation: None

Lesson:
1. This activity needs to be done on a particularly sunny day.
2. Help your child to line the shoe box with the aluminum foil.
3. Put the kabob skewer through one side of the box, through a marshmallow, and then through the second side of the box.
4. Place the plastic wrap over the top of the box.
5. Put the box in the direct sunlight and watch the marshmallow cook.

Literature -
<u>Spring song</u> by Barbara Seuling
<u>Spring thaw</u> by Steven Schnur
<u>It's spring</u> by Jimmy Pickering
<u>In the park</u> by Huy Voun Lee

Lesson One Hundred and Twenty-Five - Friday

English – Grow Your Name

Materials: Rectangular planter (or box lined with plastic)
                  Potting soil
                  Grass seeds (fast growing variety such as annual rye)

Preparation: None

Lesson:
1. Help your child to fill the planter or box with potting soil.
2. Have your child scratch out their name in the soil.
3. Have them sprinkle grass seeds into their name.
4. Have them gently cover it with soil and soon their name will be growing in the container.

Pre-Math – Counting Bugs

Materials: Index cards
                  Bug stickers

Preparation: Write numbers on each index card (1 on the first card, 2 on the second card, through the number 10)

Lesson:
1. Have your child draw a card and put the correct number of stickers on the back of each index card.
2. Let your child use these as flashcards to see if they can correctly count the stickers on each card.

Art – Paper Plate Sunflower

Materials: Paper plate
                  Yellow construction paper
                  Glue
                  Sunflower seeds or oatmeal

Preparation: Cut flower petals out of the construction paper.

Lesson:
1. Let your child glue the flower petals around the outside of their plate.
2. Let them glue the sunflower seeds or oatmeal to the inside of their flower.

Gross Motor Skills – Bumble Bee Dance

Materials: Bees, Tales from the Hive (video) – produced by Nova

Preparation: None

Lesson:
1. Watch the video with your child.
2. Have your child imitate the different bee dances.

Science – Clear Garden

Materials: Paper towel
               Clear plastic cup
               Radish seeds

Preparation: None

Lesson:
1. Have your child wet the paper towel and put it into their cup.
2. Let them sprinkle the radish seeds onto the paper towel – be sure the seeds are clearly visible.
3. Set the cups in the sun and keep the paper towel moist.
4. You will see growth in a couple of days.

Literature -
The carrot seed by Ruth Krauss
Flower garden by Eve Bunting
Holly Bloom's garden by Sarah Ashman and Nancy Parent
Lucy's secret by Mireille Levert

Week Twenty-Six

Your theme for this week will be *zoo animals*. You will be focusing on the following topics with your child:

English – The letter Z
Pre-Math – Ovals and the numbers 6-10
Art – The color black

Lesson One Hundred and Twenty-Six - Monday

English: Recognition of the Letter Z

Materials: Card stock
              Black paint
              Newspaper
              Paint smock or an old shirt

Preparation: Cut a capital letter Z out of card stock.

Lesson:
1. Have your child put on their paint smock or an old shirt to protect their clothing. Have them roll up the sleeves to minimize the mess.
2. Spread the newspapers out to protect your work surface.
3. Let your child paint black Zebra stripes on their capital Z. Let their project dry.

Pre-Math – Polar Sizes

Materials: Pictures of polar animals (see companion download)

Preparation: Print and cut out the polar animals from the companion download.

Lesson: Have your child line up the animals from smallest to largest and vice versa.

Art – Torn Paper Zoo Animals

Materials: Construction paper
Glue stick

Preparation: None

Lesson: Have your child tear piece of paper and glue them onto a large piece of construction paper to form a zoo animal or their choice.

Gross Motor Skills – Act Like a Monkey

Materials: None

Preparation: None

Lesson: Let your child pretend to be a monkey. Have him or her hop around the room making monkey noises.

Science – Blubber

Materials: 3 Ziploc bags
Shortening
Ice water

Preparation: None

Lesson:
1. Talk to your child about how animals which live in cold climates have a layer of blubber to protect them from the cold temperatures.
2. Place ice water inside two of the Ziploc bags.
3. Place shortening inside one of the Ziploc bags.
4. Put one of the ice water bags inside the bag with shortening. Seal both of these bags.
5. Spread the shortening out inside the bags so that it forms an even layer.
6. Have your child hold the bag of only ice water and see how cold that feels.
7. Now have your child hold the bag of shortening/ice water and see how cold that feels. The shortening will protect your child's hands from the cold.

Literature -
Another pet by Trisha Speed Shaskan
The baby beebee bird by Diane Redfield Massie
Charlie at the zoo by Marcus Pfister
The class trip by Grace Maccarone

Lesson One Hundred and Twenty-Seven - Tuesday

English – Giraffe "Z"

Materials: Yellow construction paper
Brown construction paper
Scissors
Two clothespins
Glue stick
Paint (optional)

Preparation: Cut out a large Z from the yellow construction paper.

Lesson:
1. Let your child cut out circles from the brown construction paper.
2. Let them glue the "spots" to their Z.
3. Have them add the clothespins to the bottom of the Z to be their giraffe's legs.
4. (optional) You can let your child paint the clothespins as well.

Pre-Math – Cookie Cutter Match

Materials: Various animal cookie cutters
Construction paper

Preparation: Trace each cookie cutter onto the paper.

Lesson: Have your child match the cookie cutters to the correct drawing on the paper.

Fine Motor Skills – Animal Lacing Cards

Materials: Animal pictures (see companion download)
Shoelace
Hole punch
Card stock

Preparation: Using the pictures in the companion download, print one or more of the animal shapes onto the card stock. Laminate the pictures and punch holes around the edges.

Lesson: Let your child lace the shoestring through the cards.

Literature -
<u>Dancing Granny</u> by Elizabeth Winthrop
<u>Do kangaroos wear seat belts?</u> by Jane Kurtz
<u>Good night, Gorilla</u> by Peggy Rathmann
<u>Lucas the littlest lizard</u> by Cathy Helidoniotis

Lesson One Hundred and Twenty-Eight - Wednesday

English: Blind Pick

Materials: Poster board or large piece of construction paper
                Thick blue marker

Preparation: Write several different numbers (1-10), letters (A-Z), and all shapes on the
                poster board with the marker.

Lesson:
1. Have your child cover their eyes and point at the poster board.
2. See if your child can identify whatever number, letter or shape they are pointing
    to.
3. Do this several times until they have identified several of the different objects.

Pre-Math – Will It Fit?!?

Materials: Bag of rice
                Tall, thin container
                Short, fat container

Preparation: None

Lesson:
1. Pour the rice into the tall, thin container.
2. Ask your child if they think the rice will fit inside the short, fat container or if it
    will spill over.
3. Pour the rice into the short container.
4. NOTE: Things that are obvious to adults are not obvious to children and are often
    hard to explain. This game is a fun activity for letting children find out about
    quantity.

Art – Paint Like a Bear

Materials: Paint
                Paper
                Old pair of socks

Preparation: None

Lesson:
1. Have your child put the socks on their hands to help them imagine not having
    fingers to use.
2. Have your child try to paint a picture with the socks on their hands.

Gross Motor Skills – Crocodiles

Materials: 3 Tbsp. margarine
                     1 bag marshmallows
                     4-6 cups Corn Flakes
                     9x13 pan
                     Non-stick pan
                     2 Sandwich-sized baggies
                     Non-stick cooking spray

Preparation: None

Lesson:
1. In a non-stick pan, help your child to melt the margarine and the marshmallows together.
2. With close supervision, your child can help to stir the mixture until the marshmallows are completely melted.
3. Then add the Corn Flakes and mix the whole thing together.
4. Have your child put the baggies on their hands. Spray the baggies with the cooking spray.
5. Let your child use the baggies to spread the mixture into the 9x13 pan.
6. When the mixture cools, cut into small rectangular or oval shapes to represent crocodile bodies.
7. Let your child enjoy the snack.

Science – Zoo Animal Numbers

Materials: 10 zoo animals (see companion download)
                     Permanent Marker

Preparation: Print the zoo animals onto paper and cut them out. Write the numbers 1-10 on each animal.

Lesson: Ask your child to line up the animal shapes from one to ten.

Literature -
Max goes to the zoo by Adria F. Klein
Miss Moo goes to the zoo by Kelly Graves
Monkey and me by Emily Gravett
My school's a zoo! by Stu Smith

Lesson One Hundred and Twenty-Nine - Thursday

English – Alphabet Zoo

Materials: None

Preparation: None

Lesson: Help your child to name a different animal which starts with each letter of the alphabet from A – Z.

Pre-Math – Monkey Board

Materials: Picture of monkey face (see companion download)
               Picture of banana (see companion download)
               Permanent marker

Preparation: Using the pictures in the companion download, print 10 copies of the monkey face and 10 copies of the banana. Write the numbers 1- 10 on each monkey face.

Lesson: Have your child place the correct number of bananas next to each monkey.

Music – Carnival of the Animals

Materials: <u>Carnival of the Animals</u> by Saint-Saëns (Music CD)
               <u>Carnival of the Animals</u> by John Lithgow and Boris Kulikov

Preparation: None

Lesson: Listen to the CD with your child. Have them dance to the music and act like the different animals that are portrayed.

Fine Motor Skills – Squishy Bag

Materials: Water
      Bowl
      4 Tbsp. cornstarch
      Food coloring
      Ziploc bag

Preparation:
1. Boil 3 cups of water.
2. In a separate bowl, add cold water to 4 Tbsp of cornstarch to make a paste.
3. Slowly add the cornstarch mixture to the boiled water.
4. Cook and stir until thick.
5. Add food coloring and allow the mixture to cool.
6. Pour the mixture into a Ziploc bag and seal it well.

Lesson: Allow your child to squish the bag without opening it. You may want to double bag the mixture to prevent accidents.

Literature -
<u>Never ever shout in a zoo</u> by Karma Wilson
<u>New at the zoo</u> by Frank B. Edwards
<u>Our class took a trip to the zoo</u> by Shirley Neitzel
<u>Polar bear, polar bear, what do you hear?</u> by Bill Martin, Jr.

Lesson One Hundred and Thirty - Friday

English – We're Going on a Zoo Hunt

Materials: We're Going on a Bear Hunt by Michael Rosen and
               Helen Oxenbury

Preparation: None

Lesson:
1. Read the book We're Going on a Bear Hunt to your child.
2. Tell your child that you're going to go hunting for different zoo animals – let them decide which animal they would like to hunt for first.
3. Act it out just like they do in the book. "We're going on a _____ hunt. We're going to catch a big one. What a beautiful day! We're not scared."

Pre-Math – All Aboard the Zoo Train

Materials: Various colors of construction paper

Preparation: Cut out "tickets" from the different colors of construction paper.

Lesson:
1. Give your child different colors of tickets.
2. Tell your child that you're the conductor of the Zoo Train and they can ride the train if they give you the correct color of ticket.
3. Set up some chairs or march around the room with your child.
4. Announce "All aboard – now taking RED tickets."
5. Have your child give you the correct color ticket and then march around the room with them.
6. After a minute, announce a new color.

Art – Create a Zoo Habitat

Materials: Leaves
               Branches
               Construction paper
               Empty paper towel rolls
               Paint

Preparation: None

Lesson: Turn your room into a zoo habitat by hanging leaves and branches from the ceiling. Let your child paint the tubes and paper to try to make the room have a jungle atmosphere.

Gross Motor Skills – Elephant Tracks

Materials: Construction paper
               Tape

Preparation: Use the construction paper to create elephant tracks. Stick them to the
               floor.

Lesson: Let your child hop from track to track.

Science – Cave Play

Materials: Blanket

Preparation: Drape a blanket over the dining room table to create a cave.

Lesson: Let your child play in their cave, read in their cave, etc.

Literature -
What would you do if you lived at the zoo? by Nancy White Carlstrom
Where will the animals stay? by Stephanie Calmenson
The Wild by Katherine Emmons
Wild about books by Judy Sierra

Made in the USA
Middletown, DE
21 February 2019